DUANE ARTHUR OSE

ALASKAN
Wilderness
ADVENTURE III

STRATTON
—PRESS—
Publishing Life

ALASKAN WILDERNESS ADVENTURE: BOOK 3
Copyright © 2019 **Duane Arthur Ose**

Stratton Press Publishing
831 N Tatnall Street Suite M #188,
Wilmington, DE 19801
www.stratton-press.com
1-888-323-7009

ISBN (Paperback): 978-1-64345-662-1
ISBN (Ebook): 978-1-64345-841-0

Printed in the United States of America

CONTENTS

INTRODUCTION

In my first book, Alaskan Wilderness Adventure, I share my venture of trekking out to find my dreamland. In the year 1985, my son Daniel and I set out to stake a claim in Alaska, to file for a federal homestead. The best way to know the land was to walk upon it. To be intimate with nature, to understand its heart and soul, like a long-married couple who have grown as one together. Dan and I walked over fifty-seven miles of unfettered Alaskan jungle, burdened with the heaviest packs we could carry and prepared for any and all emergencies. We carried enough supplies to last us a month; we were preparing to be completely on our own. We were traveling over land that had been untouched by man's destructive hand; this land was wildly alive, a virgin of untamed and pure nature. In time, I came to understand that what I thought was an erratic growth and development of the earth had a purpose with structure and design. On the fifteenth day of our journey, I found myself frozen in awe, immersed in my surroundings. It was mutual love at first sight between the land and me. As a woman, the land surrounding me seemed to speak to me, saying, "Choose me." I did just that, becoming the last homesteader to file a claim, offered by the Federal Homestead Act of 1862, a law that was signed by President Abe Lincoln.

Alaskan Wilderness Adventure II takes place in the year of 1986. That was the year I set out to build a trail leading to my dreamland. I brought along with me some muscles to help—a young lad of nineteen years of age, Jeff Peterson. With teamwork, we managed to cut our trail through the wilderness of Alaska. We constructed a three-and-a-half-mile trail to my homestead. We worked our way uphill to my chosen parcel of land, leading from my newly established base camp. Base camp was a small vacant cabin, located a quarter of a mile from the shore of a small lake. That small lake was the place used at that time for landing a plane, in which we brought ourselves and our gear. This cabin had been built in 1984 by a twenty-one-year-old Frenchman. It took him six months' time to complete construction on it and was soon after abandoned.

I decided to name the land I staked my claim Ose Mountain. Jeff and I had built a dugout dwelling during our 1986 trip. A habitable dwelling was one of the requirements by the federal government. This dwelling would need to meet the standards set by the Bureau of Land Management. That was part of the proving up process, to be awarded a land patent. A land patent is a parchment certifying the first owner of the land, which had been owned by the United States federal government before a person earning their homestead property.

Alaskan Wilderness Adventure III is an exploration of my 1987 trip to my homestead, where the goal was to continue to improve the land, as well as to begin the groundwork on my final home.

Once again, I was fortunate to have the help of another young friend, Larry Brau. Larry was twenty-one years old at the time and was also from Wood Lake, Minnesota. The goals I had set for this trip required me to bring in more tools and an ATV. These supplies would allow me to begin working on the construction of my home. I fully expected the building of the house to take several years to complete. This house would not be a weekend cabin, but an all-season, full-sized home. I was planning a dwelling that would allow me to live off the grid while supporting my future bride.

Ose Mountain is only accessible by air, so setting timely flight schedules for this trip was of the utmost importance. Safety measures were duly important. Once we were dropped off, it would be months before the next scheduled flight. Our then departure flight back to Fairbanks is on September 18.

There was a time in my life when I was a pilot. That was back in the year 1963. I never had owned a plane, which is perfectly fine by me. It is cheaper to charter flight than it would be for me to own a plane. The maintenance required for a plane is out of my price range. Too many people own a plane but seldom do any flying. Therein lays a safety risk of not being familiar enough with piloting, to keep up one's skills.

On Ose Mountain, there were no two-way communications with the outside world. We relied only on incoming radio messages. Messages were heard by tuning into a radio station. The radio station readers would open our mail that was sent to the station, then read it on-air at 9:30 p.m. every day. The letters mailed to us were addressed "In care of KJNP 1170 a.m. *Trapline Chatter*, North Pole, Alaska, 99705." Meaning we would be otherwise on our own, and the only way we could send mail at that time was by handing out letters to the pilots who were flying back to Fairbanks. We seldom sent out mail; months would pass without any unscheduled visiting pilots.

I will do my best to fill you in on the highlights that occurred during this year's visit to my homestead. There are encounters that even surprised me. It's my recollection about the Little People. These humanlike creatures in Alaska are elusive beings that live in solitude and rarely seen. I don't expect anyone to take my word for it. I am simply sharing my experiences. I feel it is my duty to do so. I come to call these beings the Hairy Ones.

Some names have been changed or omitted for protection of privacy. I wrote this book referring to my diary. During my travels between Ose Mountain, Alaska, and the Ose Farm in Minnesota, I kept a diary recounting events of each day, expounding on select portions. I also kept a video diary as well and have my home movies for recording history.

Portions of my diary are confidential and not for public knowledge.

CHAPTER 1

North to Fairbanks, Alaska

April 6

I withdrew a sufficient amount of cash from my bank account to use for my traveling to Alaska. I also exchanged US currency for a certain amount of Canadian currency. It has been my experience cash in hand speaks volumes. Checks are just paper and not accepted in most places far from home. Clearing a check through the bank while on the road takes time I didn't have. I knew nothing about credit cards, let alone a debit card. I also didn't know of any ATMs from which to withdraw money in these years.

When an American arrives at the Canadian border, there are entry inspection points they must go through. The border agents at the entry inspection points would ask me about my travel plans. They would also ask if I had a sufficient amount of cash on my person because they wanted to be sure I could fund my drive through Canada, and into Alaska, as well as having the funds to cover any car trouble that might arise. My word wasn't enough for them, and neither was proof of insurance; they demanded to see the cash. I would gander to say it was because of the way I dressed and the older pickup I drove.

Canada does not want to add foreigners to their welfare list. Those were their words, spoken to me in the past when I have crossed into Canada. That rule should apply to our southern border as well. It is a wise policy.

During this period in my life, I lived on the farm with my mother. That was after Dad had died. I spent the days before leaving for my Alaskan trip visiting with friends, to hug them and tell them my last-minute goodbyes.

April 6—the day was for doing my laundry. I wanted to have it done before my journey. I also spent time servicing my vehicle and reading through my checklist, crossing each item off, narrowing down the long list.

The air had grown heavier through the day, buzzing with tension. It reminded me of my time during the service, soldiers waiting with anticipation; you could feel the energy, the emotion as we prepared for the attack.

But this adventure brought a different challenge, overcoming Mother Nature, not only to overcome, but to adapt to it by learning, yet protecting with the love of the land—the land I called home, Ose Mountain.

April 7

I hugged and kissed Mom goodbye. Before I left, my brother, Mike, stopped by to say goodbye. Mike was a police officer in Redwood Falls, Minnesota. He assured me that he would keep an eye on things while I was gone.

I left the farm to pick up Larry Brau in the town of Wood Lake. Larry loaded his gear and his dog Susie into my truck. The truck I had back then was a King Cab Datsun pickup with bucket seats. We drove to Granite Falls to pick up the results of a medical checkup I had scheduled a few days prior. I stopped at the hospital and found the results were all clear. Thank you, God!

We had lunch at the Dairy Queen in Granite Falls, a must stop before and after each of my Alaskan trips. The time was 11:20 a.m.; the pickup's odometer read 128,793.5 miles. I started the pickup, and we headed on our way! We drove to Interstate Highway 94, which led us to North Dakota. We traveled the rest of the day, until 10:30 p.m. That night, we decided to camp in Kenmare, North Dakota.

We had traveled 504 miles when I discovered I had forgotten my laundry in Mom's dryer. I had also forgotten the owner's manual for my new Honda 350 ATV, which I had purchased about a month before on the north side of Willmar, Minnesota. "Haste makes waste," they say. At least, I had the traveling money and my test healthy results.

April 8

We left Kenmore at 6:30 a.m. and crossed into Canada. I was pulling a fully loaded, 8' x 8', small two-wheel trailer, with the ATV in it. We had to show the Canadian border guards our vaccination papers for Larry's dog, Susie, as well as the cash I mentioned before, and the proof of ownership of the ATV.

We arrived at my Uncle Loris and Aunt Dot Ose's home at 9:00 p.m. their time. They lived in Camrose, Alberta. It was late, so we camped at a campground near their home for the night. We had driven 717 miles this day. We had good weather, good roads, and made no stops at the museums, of which there were many.

April 9

We visited for a while with Loris and Dot. Then after an early dinner, we said our goodbyes, hitting the road at 11:30 a.m. I drove 431 miles that day and then paid $30 for a motel room in Fort St. John, British Columbia. We were finally on the Alaskan-Canadian Highway (ALCAN).

April 10

We left at 9:30 a.m. and drove until 7:30 p.m., gaining 424 miles on our travels this day. At a mountain side, we stopped to get close to some mountain sheep for taking pictures. We were in the scenic Canadian Rocky Mountains, where we found a campsite to stop for the night.

A and B

April 11

We broke camp and headed off for that day's journey at 7:30 a.m. We traveled until 9:30 p.m., finally stopping in the town of Beaver Creek. Located in the Yukon Territory of Canada, Beaver Creek was the last town we encountered before crossing the border into Alaska. We managed to put in 797 miles on this day. During our drive, we chanced to see three caribou; one was a nice-sized bull.

Border cut

April 12

We hit the road at 8:30 a.m., leaving Beaver Creek behind and passed through the border with no delay. Stopped to eat, and fill the pickup with gasoline at Tok, the first town in Alaska, then drove toward Fairbanks.

After I had shown Larry around the radio station, I drove him over to Santa Claus Land. Santa Claus Land was also in the town of North Pole. Later that day, we arrived in Fairbanks. That was at 4:30 p.m. We had traveled 326 miles on this day. The odometer now read 131,365 miles. That meant that from Granite Falls, Minnesota, to Fairbanks, Alaska, was 2,572 miles. We had taken the shortest route, not always on the fastest roads, but we had made a good time all the same. I think we owed our fast travel to the fact it was early in the year.

KJNP Radio

April 13

The Super 8 motel located on Airport Way in Fairbanks was $65 a night. That was a lower price than during the tourist season. Tourist season begins after the schools closed for the summer. From the motel room, I made phone calls to my brother Mike, my sister Diane Volkmann, and Mark Weronko in Anchorage.

Larry and I made visits to 40-Mile Air and Wrights Air. We set schedules with Wright Services. We learned it would take us two trips to bring all our gear out to our destination. One trip would cost me $869, the other $831. We would be flown out on a single engine, one thousand horsepower, Otter cargo plane. This plane was capable of carrying a payload up to 2,400 pounds. These two flights would bring out the supplies we needed for this year's journey, as well as some supplies to store for the future of the developing homestead.

Otter plane

CHAPTER 2

Nightlife in Anchorage

April 14

Larry and I checked out of the Super 8 motel on Airport Way. We drove down the Parks Highway, a 260-mile drive that ended in Wasilla. This trip took us about eight hours total. We did some sightseeing, which delayed our travel speed, some. We arrived at my cousin Mike E. Ose's home, located on a street off of milepost 39.5 on the Parks Highway, at the southern edge of Wasilla.

The highway going through Wasilla is of two lanes (back then in 1987) with one stop light. Wasilla was a small town but was the fastest growing community in Alaska. Mile zero, the start of the Parks Highway, was located at the northern edge of the city of Anchorage. The mile markers on this highway ended at 350 miles north, in the city of Fairbanks.

Mikey (his name of preference) was a highly skilled, well-paid pipefitter. Some of his fellow workers were at his home visiting him this evening. This crew was working on a new high school. Mikey graciously invited us to make ourselves at home.

Mikey had added on to his one-room log cabin—a cabin that my eldest son Dave and I had built in 1984. We at that time used the trees that were on his property and trees from his sister Charlene Mahoney's property, located nearby, to construct the small home.

The newly added rooms were done by modern construction material and had been built by a general contractor. The additions were a kitchen, a bathroom-laundry combination, and an upstairs bedroom. These additions turned this one-room cabin into a fully functional and complete house.

The main part of the log cabin was made from two-sided logs stacked and notched joined at the corners. The bark had been left dried and attached to the outside of the wall logs. That gave the house a rustic look. Dave and I had very little time to build this then one-room cabin, let alone time to peel logs. Mike knew this and was going to debark the walls later. Leaving the bark on gave the home a surprisingly cool and unique look. Mikey finished with the bark removal at a later date.

April 15

We woke up early and went bulk food shopping in Anchorage. We stopped by Costco, a bulk food member's only business, of which I was a member. We purchased over $1,000 in food. I always have fun shopping in a bulk store buying cases of food items, as well as other household and nonfood items. The type of shopping we were doing required careful planning, preparing for months ahead, which was all new to Larry. One personal item Larry could not go without was shampoo. He put a six-pack of shampoo on the hand cart, 15 oz. plastic bottles.

He came and asked me, "Duane, do you think that this one pack of shampoo will be enough?"

"I couldn't tell you. I never use it." So Larry added more shampoo. He grabbed two-gallon jugs and added them to the big hand cart too. (It has been 27 years now, 2014, and Rena and I still have one and three-fourth gallons of Larry's shampoo.)

My pickup's drive line shaft was making a bad noise. I drove the noisy Datsun carefully to an auto shop and replaced a center hanger bearing. The cost of the bearing and labor was $180. That evening, Mikey took Larry and me out for dinner.

April 16

Larry and I went to a nightclub early in the evening, to experience the wild Alaska nightlife. We decided to spend some time at the Bush Company One. Bush Company One is in the old part of Anchorage. The second Bush nightclub, Bush 2 Company, is in the newer part of Anchorage. Both are adult entertainment clubs. The buildings are vastly different from each other but still very much like the early days of saloons in Alaska. I am not sure, but I think the bars in Alaska remain open until 3:00 a.m. and then reopen soon after.

There are signs at the entrances of the bars that read "No guns allowed." Like that of a hat check room, guns were checked in before you could have your fun, then returned as you were leaving. At some bars in the remote country areas, you simply lock the gun in your vehicle. Here in Anchorage, when you enter the lobby of an adult entertainment club, you will notice that it is like that of a lobby found in a movie theater. Each one warmly greeted and might be asked for proof of age. They want to see what type of mood you're in, by your response. They also wanted to know of anyone armed.

We passed through the lobby check station and let our eyes become acclimated to the low light inside of the club. We worked our way to a small round table with four empty chairs, located near a low stage floor. On this stage, women were performing special, alluring, exotic, seductive acts, as well as pole dancing. Music was playing, and there were multiple colored lights flashing on the entertainers.

We were immediately waited on by a seductively dressed waitress in high heels. She asked me, "What will you have, sir?" and bending close to my face. I found my eye momentarily gazing at her loosely fitted top, smelling her intoxicating fragrance. For an instant, I found myself stuttering. I remembered to breathe and gave her my order.

The waitress slowly turned away from me and faced Larry to take his order. I was not looking at the stage during this time. I had my eye fixed on this waitress, facing away from me, with her high heels, short skirt, and low-cut top. She turned to me and said with a smiley wink, "I will be right back," as she pranced off fluidly, like a tiger on the hunt.

Larry leaned in close to me and with a smile on his face said, "I like this place already."

"Tonight, I am buying, Larry, enjoy."

The waitress brought us our drinks, and I said, "Keep the change."

"Thank you, sir. Looks to me you men could use a lap dance."

Larry turned and asked me, "What's a lap dance?" Before I could explain, two beautiful ladies approached us. It was a good thing the room was warm, or they would be cold for the lack of, and sheerness, of the clothing they wore.

"Nice heels," I told the older of the two.

"Thank you," she said. Raising one leg, she placed her foot on my right knee so that I could have a closer look at the classy shoe. Steadying herself with her hand on my left shoulder, she brought her foot back to the floor. "I felt your strong muscles. I like a man that keeps in shape."

"You look to be firm too."

She took my right hand and placed it on her thigh. "Feel my legs." I did as she said, running my hand up, down, and around, feeling her firm legs.

"Wow, nice!" I said. "What's your secret?"

From this point on, Larry was left on his own. I thought he could manage without me. He had a woman sitting on his lap.

The woman, who had stayed in my company, glanced over at Larry. She went on to tell me that she and her friend were country girls. "We like horseback riding, camping, hiking, fishing, and target practicing with rifles."

"Hey, we girls came over to you guys to see if you'd like a lap dance, how about it?"

"Okay, great! Sure! As soon as I have this $100 bill made to change. And for your friend, here's another hundred to change." I needed to give Larry some ammo. I winked at her. She took my money and waved it high toward the female cashier.

In short order, a gal came over and broke the money down for me. I handed half to Larry. "Have fun. Buy some lap dances, Larry."

The girls had us move back away from the table while remaining on our chairs. "Okay, now what?" I asked.

"We're going to dance for you. There is one rule, though."

"What's that?"

"No touching. You just sit there and let us take over."

"Larry! You hear that?"

"Loud and clear," Larry said.

I looked around. I saw there were lone customers and whole groups of married couples, all sharing a good night out enjoying their lap dancers too. Seeing everyone was having a good time helped me realize I was doing nothing different from anyone else. I was feeling very comfortable.

To view a dancer on stage was one thing. But having my personal dancer, to dance just for me, doing her numbers up close, cannot be compared. She started out in front of me, going through her dancing routine. She made constant eye contact with me as I looked at more of her than just her eyes and back up to meet her eyes. She was playing with me, reading my mind, seeing what pleased me most of all. Then she would concentrate on that pleasurable dance move. Her dancing was driving me crazy.

The cocktail waitress returned, and I indicated to her to bring us another round, plus drinks for the dancers. My lap dancer said, "Thanks. I could use a cold drink right now."

The dancer with her attention on me placed her hands on my knees, spreading my legs wide at that point. She worked her swaying, dancing, luscious body, in gently between my spread legs. She wasn't touching me, but I could feel her closeness, and her aura, all the same. You know, that field of energy that emits when you're close to a wall, and you cannot see in the dark.

The drinks were then on the table between Larry and me, within reach of the four of us. I paid and tipped the waitress. While passing by, the waitress stopped and whispered in my ear, "I want to give you a lap dance the first opening I get, honey," and deliberately rubbed against my leg as she moved away.

The lap dances they gave were lengthy but left us wanting more and more. Each dance, we tucked greenbacks in their tight waistline string. (Well, there were no pockets. Where else could we place the money?) Inserting the bills was a fun part for all four of us, an opportunity to touch.

The girls pulled up a chair and sat beside us. We visited like we were old friends. My dancer talked to her friend, and then to me. "Excuse us, we need to go to the powder room. Promise us you will wait here, please? We will be back real soon."

"Ladies, the only place we might go is to the men's room. So if we're not here when you get back, wait for us." They headed off for the powder room.

Almost as soon as our girls were out of sight, the waitress and another gal came over to us. "Hey, honey, I told you I would be giving you a lap dance! Sit back and relax. We're going to give you some real dances."

Before things progressed any further, I explained, "The girls just went to the powder room. They're coming right back."

"Not a problem, we're here now."

These girls were aggressively grinding us with their lap dancing routines, like Amazons. I never dreamt lap dancing could be even more intoxicating than what we had already experienced. Wow! I glanced at Larry and saw he was about to go freaky. It was as if he was about to lose self-control and break the rules of behavior.

"Larry! Have a drink. Put some ice on it."

Larry came back by saying, "The ice is evaporating," as he laughed out loud.

When the first girls came back, things became interesting, to say the least. Still, diplomacy prevailed. My lap dancer was sounding a wee bit cool and asked me, "Was she good for you?"

"Yes, but I prefer you. I'm glad you're back." In no time, everything was back to normal. I could feel the tension hanging there, but for only a lingering moment.

After another lap dance, silently, the girls took us by our hands. They lead us to an alcove—an L-shaped booth, off in an isolated corner. There was a wall at our backs and to one side of us. We could still see the stage, but not much more of the club.

This booth was nice, soft, and comfortable. A place where we could have a relaxing snuggle. It meant that we were in a semi-private comfort zone. My gal and I slid back deep into the corner. No one could see this part of the booth unless a person deliberately would approach the booth to serve us.

It wasn't until this moment that the four of us properly introduced one another. My new friend's name was Jenny. Her girlfriend's name was Anna. They were still on the clock, so we had to continue buying lap dances and drinks, or they would have to move on to find new paying customers.

Besides being cozy, they were asking to know about us. When they heard of our upcoming adventure into the wilderness, that we were planning on being there five full months and weren't returning until September, the girls didn't bat an eye. Instead, they raised their eyebrows and asked for more information.

Jenny and Anna were totally countries. They lived up in the Matsu Valley, near Wasilla and Palmer, about forty miles up the road. They were renting a small apartment by the month and were actively looking for a better place. When they weren't working the hours at the club, they rented horses at a Wasilla Ranch and rode up into the mountains on trial rides. They loved all aspects of the outdoors and knew how to use their firearms.

The conversations led to them wanting to know more about our adventure. They were showing increasing interest in accompanying us. I wanted them to understand what to expect. I explained to them lodging there was a small dugout, with two three-foot wide rope bunk beds. There was only a brief pause before Jenny said, "It sounds cozy." They still wanted to come along!

"Where are you hanging now, while you're in town?" Jenny asked.

"At my cousin's place, outside of Wasilla, but the four of us can't go there tonight. Where's your place?" Jenny told us, but it might as well have been in a foreign language to me. "I would get lost. I don't know addresses very well." I knew how to get to Mikey Ose's home, and the nearby places, but that was my range of familiarity with the area.

"How about we meet in a place I know, and we'll follow you from there? Jenny, there is the small matter of this job and your belongings?"

"That's not a problem. We have friends who let us store our few big items. As for the job, we can come back to it anytime. We're not about to miss out on this once in a lifetime opportunity."

"We are off the clock in about an hour, at 2:00 a.m. Where would you like to wait for us?"

"How about the place the locals call the Store?" The Store was a twenty-four-hour gas station on the Parks Highway and this side of Wasilla.

"Perfect! We know it well, and it's not far from where we live. Did you say we'd be flying out from Fairbanks the day after tomorrow?"

"Yup, the first flight is set for 10:00 a.m."

"Oh boy, we have some packing to do! Could you help us? It will be small things like clothes, our hiking gear, guns, and our personal things."

"Jenny, it would work best if you and Anna followed us up to Fairbanks tomorrow morning. I will rent a motel room for us that night. That way, you'd have your car up there in Wright's storage parking lot, kept safe until you need it come September. Or if you get tired of us, and the wilderness."

Jenny and Anna looked at each other a moment, then Anna said, "That's a good backup plan, but we have a feeling that this is the beginning of a beautiful relationship. For sure, an adventure we want to be a part of."

"Okay, then."

Jenny went on to tell us they both they liked to cook, so they would make sure we're bringing in enough food. They were going to help us go over our lists the following day. We knew we could finish shopping for any more items we needed in Fairbanks.

After a lingering hug, Larry and I headed out to wait for the girls at the appointed place.

Larry and I went inside the Store and bought some soda and munchies to snack on while we waited in the pickup. We first parked up front under the lighted area, near the highway's off-ramp. A state trooper slowly cruised by, checking us out. He saw if we were up to no good. We weren't. Still, to avoid being hassled, we decided to move to a shadowed spot, next to the store. I parked with the motor off facing the off-ramp, and we waited for them to roll in. My plan was to put the headlights on and drive up to them, once they appeared in the lighted area.

This part was not discussed very well between Jenny and me. All I had said was that we would be waiting there. I had forgotten that this store and gasoline station was a busy place filled with cars. I should have remembered how long it takes some women to get ready. It seemed like hours passed by while we waited eyes fixed on the off-ramp.

Larry spoke first. "I don't think they're coming."

"You're probably right, Larry, we are saps. Like young scouts trying to bag snipes in a snipe hunt at night."

I was outside the pickup headed for the men's room, when Larry yelled, "*Here they come!*" I turned to see Jenny and Anna driving down the off-ramp into the lighted area. I scrambled back into the cab as quick as I could, to drive up to them. Their car had driven in only a short ways, stopped a moment, and then just as quickly backed out. They turned around and drove off, all before I could do anything. They disappeared into the dark of night, gone, disappearing down the dark road. Dang!

They never even drove around to look for us. I suppose with the amount of time that had passed, they must have thought we skipped out on them. Why didn't we just stay in the lighted area? Dang! I didn't think to write down the address Jenny had given me. I didn't have a phone number either. I only knew where they worked. It would be years before I would be back in there. So, Jenny and Anna, if you should find yourselves reading this, I'm sorry. It was not meant to be.

"I don't think we would have gotten any work done," Larry said.

CHAPTER 3

The Longest Day

April 17

We woke up early, having stayed the night at Mickey's house. We wanted to make sure and have time to say our goodbyes before heading out. We had our breakfast and then hit the road headed back up to Fairbanks. We arrived at Wrights Air at 4:00 p.m. I confirmed the arrangements with Wrights Air to fly out at 10:00 a.m. the next morning. We checked into the Klondike Inn for the night. I made a phone call from the room to my brother Mike and had him forward the information about my hotel and room number, to share with Mom and David. I received my final phone call (next call would be in September) from Mom and David around 2:00 a.m. Alaska time. It was five in the morning there in Minnesota.

April 18

We were up bright and early, at 6:30 a.m. We took our last shower until we returned, wrote and mailed some letters, paid the phone bill of $5, and checked out. McDonald's was our choice for breakfast, before purchasing the remainder of our goods. We bought twenty gallons of gasoline at the bulk plant, in five-gallon cans. We drove to the airport and unloaded the bulk food, our gear, and the twenty gallons of gasoline. We were right on schedule for our 10:00 a.m. departure to basecamp. I parked the pickup in the secured parking lot of Wrights Air. The tools and supplies we had hauled up from Minnesota had already been loaded on the plane.

I went out on the first flight, along with the Honda ATV, and enough other supplies to fill the plane. About one to one and a half hours later, we landed on the lake. The lake's shallow snow cover on the ice was in excellent shape; no snow melting had begun yet. The snow cover was not deep, and it made for a good ski landing. The temperature was comfortable and only needed a light jacket.

I set the tripod up and mounted the camcorder. I had the lens pointed toward the shoreline, directing it where I would be completing my task of assembling the trailer. I was busy mounting the tires and bolting down the trailer's box, when suddenly I realized I was not alone. I heard a voice call out, "Hello, you must be Duane Ose." I looked to shore and saw a tall man approaching me from my trail. He was without a coat, and his hands were empty. All the while, the VHS camcorder was rolling.

Me and ATV on the lake

"Yes, I am. How do you know my name?"
"Your name is on the door up there."

Name on door

I thought to myself, *That's a bit fishy. He pronounced my last name (Ose) correctly.* That is unusual; no one gets it right the first time. The Ose name is pronounced, O-C. "You have me at a disadvantage. You know my name, what is yours?" He had walked right up to me at this point.

"Sam Connor. I was flown out to this lake five months ago. I still have some gear over there." He pointed to the northeastern part of the lake, where there was a small plywood cabin that was not his.

"My land claim is northwest of here, at a junction of two creeks."

"What two creeks? There is only one small creek up that way," I said.

"You're right, only marsh grasses. On the topo map, however, it shows waterway lines."

"So, Sam, you only paper claimed and had not physical visited the land before hand?"

"Well, yes, but the map at the BLM office showed where the claims already staked were, so I did not file on top any of the already taken lands."

"Sam, you're supposed to buy that map, as well as see the land in person. Not just put your finger on the map and then write in your claim. Sam, how did you come to finding my place?"

He went on to tell me, "I had been dropped off here midwinter, and it was cold. That small plywood shack was taking too much wood to heat. So I looked around all the lakes for a cabin to use until I could build mine. That is when I saw the land I had claimed was a bad choice because of its location. It was shortly after that I came across your trail. I followed it up, and there was this nice dugout. It looked easy to heat with the firewood cut and stacked too."

"How did you get in?"

"That took some thinking. I figured it was a trick door. I looked high up at that wooden burl near the door, figured that had to play a part in its operation. So I spun it until the door handle let me pull the door open. After that, I moved in."

(Note here: It was a trick door, and the wood burl was meant to be pulled outward, not turned. It must have worked as well by turning it, though. It had wound the cord, raising the locking toggle. That allowed the door latch to be raised by pulling the handle and pulling the door open. I had not counted on an intelligent thinker to figure out how the door worked. I had assumed any trespassers would not try to open it. Sam, apparently, was desperately seeking shelter.)

"Sam Conner, where do you come from?"

"Texas. I hitchhiked up to Alaska a couple of years back. I found a summer job on an experimental farm, which was growing potatoes in the delta flats." (The delta flats are a fertile location used for farming.) Sam went on to tell me, "I heard about this settlement area, filed a claim, and bummed a flight here. I was expecting to find a lot of settlers (sixty-four). Now I am relocating my claim just a few yards away from your place."

Oh great! I thought to myself.

All the while, I was assembling my trailer, while he just pranced around, getting colder by the minute. I sighed and pointed out a long leather coat draped on my pile of things. "Put that on, Sam, and my raccoon hat. I am expecting the second otter plane shortly, with Larry and his dog."

Sam, when he heard that, responded by saying, "I better get back up there to make room," and left.

"Wow, man! You are bringing in a lot of stuff."

I couldn't help, but think, *Yup, he is a certified hippy flower child.* Not that matters but depends on the person.

I had no time to think about the mess awaiting us up at my dugout, so went on about preparing for the second load.

I had modified an axle for this trailer, according to my specs and done by a welder who was an employee at Seaforth Salvage in Seaforth, Minnesota. I had used my father's old, junked out, Case Combine's six-inch axle, its sixteen-inch wheels, and six ply tires. I had shortened the axle so that after the wheels were on along with the sixteen-inch Combine tires, it would be four feet wide. The same width as an ATV 4×4, for the trails I had already made, and those I would be making.

That was no ordinary axle trailer set up, but I had constructed it for multipurpose uses:

1. It would be for bolting on a plywood trailer box sized two feet wide by five feet long by two feet high.
2. With the trailers box removed, an axle assembly would be used for hauling logs up to sixty feet in length, or a combination of logs that fitted between the tires, supported on the axle, and whatever the weight the ATV was able to pull.
3. I had made a twenty-foot-long wooden framed road grader by using a four-foot wide steel snow blade from an ATV snow dozer attachment.

In the latter years, I built that improvised road grader for the final grading and grooming of an airfield. The setting for the blade's height was made adjustable by affixing a ¾" × 4" stud bolt to be extended or shortened as needed, levering the arch up or down of the main pole that extended from end to end of the grader. The final setting, when hooked up to the ATV, was set at the level of the level plain of the ground. That meant the rear wheels of the ATV to the blade to the rear wheels were the same level. This setting of the blade's height was meant for cutting the high points, dozing the excess soils to drop into the lows. There was just enough give in the wood pole to allow freedom of bending until the surfaces became graded level.

Repeating this grading until the blade no longer was cutting but only touching the planned surface, the result would be a smooth level airfield. This airfield would be on top of my mountain. This level plain (airfield) would afford me access twelve months of the year versus nine months on a lake or river.

The trailer axle with its telescopic adjustable reach pole had a wide range of limits to make a longer reach pole for some extremely long house logs. I made a reach pole from a tamarack tree that could be inserted into the square tubing of the original reach pole and bolted.

Tamarack trees are a slow growing tree; its growth rings are very small. Tamarack is a member of the pine family but is unlike all other pine. This tree turns brown, shedding its needles in the fall. Tamarack trees are free of knots, the stronger of the trees, and in the past were used as masts for sailing ships.

The heavy gauge, six-inch axle with implemented tires would keep the logs off the ground. The high clearance would work well in the rough and boggy terrain.

After the assembly, I hooked the trailer frame up to the Honda ATV. I pulled it around to pass in front of the camcorder. The kid in me performed a few wheelies before coming to a stop. When I came to a stop, I heard the drone of the Otter plane in the distance approaching the lake. The sound of an otter plane is very distinct. It makes a sort of *putter-putter*, a sound like three boards slapping the air—somewhat like that of a helicopter.

I dismounted the camcorder and held it on my shoulder, recording the landing. The pilot, Harold Griffin, was bringing the powerful plane down, gliding on the snow-covered ice toward me with the greatest of ease. After the plane had touched down, the pilot brought it right up to my side. He slowed the engine and then shut the engine off. I remounted the camcorder to the tripod while keeping it rolling. I walked up to the plane's wide, sliding door.

The door opened, and Harold hung out the metal ladder to the bottom of the door. Larry climbed out, followed by his dog Susie.

Larry helped me spread out a large blue tarp on the snow, on which to place the supplies. We made an assembly line. Harold would hand down items to Larry and me, and we would pile everything on the tarp. The camcorder was still on and recording this offloading. Susie was busy running all around, and once in a while, Larry would toss her a snowball to keep her entertained.

Larry, Suzie, and plane

"That's all of it," Harold said. We struck up a conversation about the wildlife out here and in Denali Park. Denali Park's property line is only fifteen miles east of Levi Lake, the lake used as a landing strip. Harold knew a lot about the moose and wolf population in these areas. Harold told us about the drastic drop in the moose population in my area, over the recent years. According to him, and he would know, there used to be an abundance of moose here. He said the Fish and Game Wildlife Management were to blame, for saving the wolves in the park. Harold was very adamant about the differences he had noticed after the controlled hunting of the overpopulated wolves had ended.

The Denali National Park is a protected zone for the wolves; they are free to kill moose wherever they find moose whether inside the boundaries of the park or not. We agreed that when man interferes with the laws of nature, after a few years, there becomes an imbalance in the habitat. Protecting all the wolves changed the predator versus prey ratio, leaving less and less moose meat, and more meat eaters.

When the moose sources are depleted, the wolves won't starve out, or also termed crash. Instead, they will move to find a different moose population. I can understand hunting to eat, but when moose are abundant, wolves hunt for pleasure. They eat only select parts of a moose or even nothing at all. Nothing goes to waste, however. There are plenty of scavengers taking advantage of the needless kills.

The wolves expand outward in search for more to eat or kill until they reach a point where the food isn't readily available. That is when they began to eat each other to survive, and eat that last moose. Trappers and hunters are the better in keeping the balance, knowing when the wolf numbers are brought back to a sustainable, healthy balance. Experienced trappers know the signs of when the animals have been overtrapped and will adjust the number of animals they catch accordingly. That keeps enough breeding stock to replenish the animals, resulting in consistent healthy catches the following year.

Like anything, though, we trappers must not become greedy, like the killer wolf, trapping out the last of our sported animals. That can apply to any marketable fur in the land. Slob trappers (not prudent trappers) trap like the roving hungry wolf and abandon a trapped out area, only to move to a new area, clear harvesting area by area. It is fine to expand a trapping area, or rest an area, but never should overtrap an area. Wolves are smart, but man can be smarter. Man is part of nature and plays a key role.

Before Harold left, he gave me some valuable advice. If I kept gasoline cans at my destination, they could be filled from the plane's on-board fuel tanks, thus leaving me more space on the plane for other supplies. At the time, all I had were five-gallon cans. In the future, I planned to leave fifteen- and fifty-five-gallon drums at the drop-off location, to utilize his suggestion.

We shook hands, and I handed him a VHS tape in an envelope to mail. We said our goodbyes, and he was off, headed back to Fairbanks. I filmed the plane powering up and then taking to the air.

Plane taking off

I decided to inform Larry that we had company. I figured it was the right time to inform Larry about our new neighbor. "Larry, we have a neighbor. His name is Sam Connor, and he was just here when you flew in. He seems to be an okay guy, but I have some serious doubts about his ability to hack it out here. He had made himself at home in my dugout a few months before us coming out here. It's been an interesting introduction, to say the least. When he heard the second plane, and I told him you were coming to join us, he scampered back up to my dugout to clean house and make space for us. I'll be just surprised as you are to see what mess awaits us and had taken up residency in the dugout." Larry was a man of few words, but I could see he was thinking about what I said.

"Who knows, we might get some work out of him, but I'm not betting on it."

After we had completed all the hard work of unloading the plane and it had flown off, Sam decided to show up. It didn't take a mule's kick to my head to figure out Sam was a freeloader.

After our introductions, Larry and Sam headed up to the dugout. I had instructed them to clear a path of any obstacles that would slow me down while pulling the trailer load.

There were about twelve inches of soft snow on the trail to plow through. Traveling on the level portions of the trail was no problem.

On the inclined slopes, however, I found myself unhooking the trailer and driving upslope like a madman. I had to do this so I would not get stuck, or spin out of the trail. I used my ATV like a plow to clear the way. That enabled me to drive back down, rehook the loaded trailer, and pull it up the slopes without a problem.

ATV on trail

There would be several days of hauling supplies. The food was the first items we transported, followed by loads carrying supplies that were a lesser priority. Most black bears were in hibernation; otherwise, the bear damage would have been the biggest threat in leaving the supplies left unattended on the lake.

Black bears tend to stay in their winter dens until melting snow or rain begin to drip on them. Grizzly bears are a different matter. They are not true hibernators. They can wake up on any warmer day, and stroll about, hungry for a snack.

This day had been a long day already, but it looked to be longer. Having a squatter using my place while I was gone was not in the plan. I can understand taking shelter in a time of need. To have someone arbitrarily move into a complete stranger's house did not set well with me. What's more, he thought nothing of it when confronted.

I agreed to let him stay the night because of the time of the year. I was diplomatic about it, telling him tomorrow he would need to pack up and find someplace else or use his tent. During the ensuing conversations, I learned how he came to pronounce my last name correctly. Sam just happened to show up each night at suppertime at the Hannans' place, some eight walking miles from my place. Yes, even with a family of four, they were generous enough to feed Sam.

In fact, from conferring with the Hannans' later on, my good neighbors told him I was coming back in early spring. Sam had decided after that to use my place while he ever so slowly worked at building his cabin and within the sound of a snoring distance from my door. The whole of thirty thousand acres and he chose to settle right next to me. It wasn't even a legal claim. Needless to say, he was a certified freeloader.

That night, Larry and I slept in the bunk beds, and Sam slept curled up on the floor with his things around him.

CHAPTER 4

Trouble Is Brewing

April 19

awoke to dogs barking and making whimpering sounds. "Sam, are those your dogs? They sound starved!"

"Yeah, I have two on leashes at my camp. After I eat breakfast, I will feed them."

"*No!* You will feed them now!" It turns out, Sam had only brought two, twenty-five-pound bags of dog food and was about to run out. The dogs never were allowed to be loose or run about at all. They were kept chained up 24-7. I thought to myself, *Why?*

Before noon, Sam walked down to the Hannans' for Easter Sunday dinner, leaving his dogs behind. He walked by direct trail over the frozen lakes. This summer, he would have to walk around the lakes that he walked on now to their places.

Later Sam was telling us of the wonderful people that lived down there. "They're so good to me," he said. Oliver Cameron, an elderly man, and the family of four, the Hannans.

There was no trading of help; he was a taker. Not only was he almost out of dog food, but he was also living off a nearly empty bag of pancake mix, and of course from his neighbors. The writing was on the wall. If he weren't about to work for food, he would have to find a way back to town. I had plenty of food to share and would gladly feed him and his dogs, but not without him helping me. I have no doubt that even ever after he returned to town, it would be straight to a food shelter. He was clearly not the sort willing to seek out a paying job. There was only laziness in his mind, and I had no sympathy for him. There was not a physical thing wrong with Sam.

I spent the rest of the day hauling supplies up from the lake. During one of my trip down at the lake, a plane landed. There were a man and a woman looking for Oliver, and the Hannans. I pointed the way, and they were off. I never was told their names, nor did I ask.

Larry spent all day washing dishes and cleaning up after Sam. Sam had never washed the dishes in all the time he spent in my dugout. He was a disrespectful, uninvited guest. The dugout was a pigsty. He even used all my firewood and cut the nearby trees for more firewood. He even cut down some wet green trees.

That evening, Larry and I were listening to KJNP Trapline chatter. Suddenly, the door opened and in walked Sam. It was well after sunset. "What's to eat?" he boldly asked.

"Let's make some popcorn." That was my idea. That way Sam would have a full belly, and we would have a treat too. Since it was late, I let him spend the night. I could then hear Larry muttering to himself, and perhaps I was too. I never, in all my life, have known anyone like him. I could feel the friction building. Sam had a perfect sense of timing when it came time to eat or sleep.

April 20

Sam moved his belongings out of my dugout. Other than that, it was an uneventful day. Larry made a gut-stuffing supper, and to our surprise, Sam did not drop in for a bite. There were no messages for us on the radio that night. We just sat around relaxed and stayed up late. Mostly we were talking about Sam, and what we might expect from him next. We agreed there was potential for him becoming a problem someday, given his character.

For the next few days, nothing eventful occurred, just the normal day-to-day happenings and Sam. His mooching was starting to wear on my last nerve. Something had to change. I went over to

Sam's camp one day and had a stern talking with him. Among other things, I told him to find another way to get to his camp, rather than to use my trail. I was kind enough, however, to haul his two dog dishes up from the lake that his dogs loved. I would have thought in all the months that had gone by, with him walking by empty-handed, his stuff every time he went to have supper at the Hannans, that he would have had all his gear at his camp long ago. Sam was the poster child for laziness.

In time, Larry and I had the 7" TV (a DC 12-volt), and the car radio is working fairly well through their antennas. We even had VHS movies to watch at night, or at least when we had charged the batteries. To our surprise, we could get a couple of TV stations clearly, and a few more that were shadows of shows, using only rabbit ears on the TV. The shows were coming from Anchorage, which is about three hundred miles to the south of Ose Mountain. It seems the analog signals bounced off Denali Mountain and back down to us. I decided the next trip is hauling a big all channel TV antenna.

With the skip on the CB, we could talk to other people. Some people were fishing at sea, or the natives that lived far to the northern lands of Alaska, some were located in parts of British Columbia, Anchorage, and even on the top of a downtown Tokyo hotel in Japan.

April 23

One thing that happened April 23, I almost lost my life to a dead tree. I was driving rather fast and had nearly reached the lake, just past the Frenchman's cabin. As I rounded a sharp corner, one of the hard, pointy, small tamarack trees had fallen, but not quite all the way to the ground. Like a spear, it passed under my ATV's windshield and struck me below my ribs on my left side. The impact pushed me back on the Honda's seat. This tree could not have been better placed lying in wait for me.

The tip of this fire-hardened dead tree was undamaged, except for the small branches involved in the collision. Those were shaved off. It had gone through my Levi's jacket, through my heavy shirt, and penetrated my skin. Blood was spilling. I removed the splintered wood that was sticking in me and used my handkerchief to stop the bleeding. No broken ribs. I closed my shirt with the handkerchief on my wound and went on to load the trailer.

April 25

I had completed hauling the supplies up from the lake and began working on building the smokehouse. Along with our work, we were both fighting off colds. We must have brought the virus in with us because we had not had contact with anyone else that could have passed us the germs while we were out there.

It had been seven days since we arrived, and there were yet no letters read to us on KJNP Radio. It was hard to get used to this lack of letters from home. Being the big sissies we were, we would say this comment to make light of our situation: "No one loves us anymore." Even though we knew that it took time for letters to get to North Pole, Alaska, Larry missed getting no mail more than me. It was his first time being so far from home, close friends, and in the general proximity of other people.

To be a weekend camper alone is one thing, but for a long time alone, it takes a lot of adjusting. The best way to handle this is to keep busy and not dwell on the fact of being alone. I wasn't confident Larry would be able to adjust. During our working hours, he was fine, but at night, he struggled more. When he didn't get any letters, you could see he was feeling down, a real kicked in the butt emotion. I am not sure Larry will be able to adjust. During the working hours, he is fine. That would change in the days to come.

I had started to notice there was an absence of wildlife in our proximity since we arrived. I didn't see any gray jays or my one squirrel friend. It wasn't long before I discovered Sam had a semi-automatic 18-round .22cal rifle and had been busy shooting anything that moved, even small birds.

Sam also had a big game rifle, but I think in a short time, he ran out of bullets for it and used the .22 rifle. The last I heard him use the big game rifle was when he recklessly killed a bear next to our outhouse at night. Every day, Sam would hunt for food, ranging far and wide. Even with that food source, he was relying on mooching off his neighbors often. Eight miles wasn't enough to keep him away for long.

It was ten at night, and Larry and I were in the dugout. We were just relaxing for the night when we heard *zip, zip* followed by sounds of two shots from a high-powered rifle. *Boom! Boom!* (The zipping sound was from the bullets tearing through the air past the dugout.)

"What the heck, what is that kid up to now?"

The air was still and silent; the shooting seemed to be over. I went out to investigate, and then by the outhouse, I saw a medium-sized black bear lying dead.

The bear had been running from Sam's camp toward ours. He shot the bear as it was heading toward my dugout. We were in the line of fire. One bullet passed through the bear and whizzed on past the dugout. The other missed the bear and ripped on really close to us.

The bear was about 150 pounds, and we were not about to help him. We went back to bed; it took Sam all night to skin it. I think he wanted us to do the work by making the time drag on and on. He would be wrong; it is Sam's kill and his responsibility, and after all, he was now paying for his recklessness. It will be a lesson to him hopefully.

Bear hide and tent

Later on, Sam brought that dried bear hide to us to trade for 250 pounds of dog food, which we did have. First trading he ever did,

I was shocked. Sam paying for his food, as well as food for his dogs, was something I hadn't expected. After Sam had killed that bear, he made his dogs happy having meat to eat. He even shared some with us as we tried to be civil the best we could, given the circumstances.

From time to time, I would ask Larry to go over to Sam's camp to check on him and his dogs. It was never a good report. There was never any good progress made on the building of his cabin. Four posts in the ground, with four logs around on top the posts, making the base of what would be a very small cabin, should he finish it. My guess is it was eight feet by ten feet long.

Sam's cabin log

Sam's tools were one single bit ax and a cheap, dull bow saw. Nothing more but what he could bum off others. I lent him a hammer and a three-fourth-inch diameter, twenty-foot length of rope for him to pull by hand his cabin logs. The nails I gave him.

Sam's shelter was a small tent with no room for his food or supplies. They were left on the ground unprotected. Sam was unprepared to live outside in the cold winter and early spring and looked around for shelter of existing cabins. In his search found mine by following my cut trail leading up from the lake. There were three other cabins, but he chose the best one; that one was mine. So until I arrived at the lake in April, he had been living in my dugout.

His days consisted of getting up at noon and then eating pancakes while his two dogs spent their time chewing on raw black bear bones of the bear he had shot. Sam's hunting was no more than a walkabout; that consisted of him shooting with his 22. rifle anything that moved, even the cheerfully singing small songbirds that were uneatable, or nonsubstantial.

We shared the same drinkable spring water source like in the days of old.

Flowing spring

For drinking water, I had improved a flowing spring, coming from the base of our hill some three hundred yards away. I had tapped into it with a three-fourth-inch poly length of hose to get the pure water before it rose to the surface and became contaminated. The outlet of the hose emptied far out in a cluster of willows. That water system was used for us three for water. The friction between Sam and us was so great that we made it a point to never collect water at the same time.

Around noon that day, I heard one shot, followed in the next moment by seventeen rapid fire shots from what had to have been Sam's .22cal semi-auto rifle. The bangs came from below in the wooded box canyon. He, for whatever reason, had unloaded his rifle on something. I thought no more of it until that night.

At supper, as we ate, I brought the shooting up to Larry. Larry said, "I will go over there tonight and see what Sam is up to."

"Okay, but be careful, Larry."

A short time later, he came back with this report. With great disgust, Larry told me that Sam had killed a moose, a cow moose.

"*What?*"

"Yup, he did." Larry went on to explain about his walk over to Sam's camp and the talk that ensued.

"When I got to Sam's camp, he was carrying a large piece of moose on his back, up the steep hill."

"What the heck happened? June is the month when things start getting warm; this is no time to be shooting big game without a means of canning it or freezing it."

"That's what I said too."

Larry went on to tell me about what Sam had said to him. Sam had been emphasizing how big of a hunter he was and being thrilled from his kill.

"Sam told me he was going down for water with the water bucket in one hand, and the .22 in the other. As he was walking, this big cow moose stepped right out in front of him, real close, then stood there looking down at him. He said he aimed for her eyeball, put the first bullet in her eye, and then emptied the rest into her head. The moose only staggered about two steps, before falling to the ground. Since the time he shot her, he had been cutting and bringing up the meat. By the time I got there, Sam was working on bringing up the last of the meat. He told me his plan was to slice the meat into thin strips, then hang it out on racks to dry. He was planning on making jerky."

Larry told me he then asked Sam, "Have you ever done this before, making jerky?"

Sam replied with "No, but I have heard of how to."

I asked Larry, "What did you do then?"

"Nothing, I just shook my head and came on back."

"Of all the people in this world, and way out here in the middle of nowhere, how did we end up with such an idiot neighbor as Sam Connor?"

*   *   *

About a week had passed, when Larry and I went over to check on Sam, and this time, we came armed. It was like in the movies. "We smell the dump, and now where is the village?" We confronted Sam, who was, by the way, in his tent on top of a platform high off the ground, a platform meant for storing his food.

The whole area stank to high heaven and the big flies were everywhere. Dogs were barking from having the biting flies on them.

"Hey, Sam, I see you're safe way up there!"

Sam, looking all sleepy eyed, opened his tent that had been keeping him safe from the meat-eating flies. It was so sad that it was all we could do to hold back our anger.

Sam said, "It's safe up here. There is a bear around that's why I have the tent up here."

"No wonder," I said. "Get rid of the rotting meat. It's a bear and fly magnet."

Larry and I left to return to our dugout.

*   *   *

Some days later, the Federal Bureau of Land Management inspectors flew in to inspect my dwelling, to see if I had qualified for granting me a land patent. They walked up, did their inspection, and walked on back out, flying back to Fairbanks.

After they had left, Sam asked me, "Did they approve you?"

"Yes, they did, Sam,"

Sam responded with "They didn't pass me."

"So they told me, Sam."

The final straw that made me put my foot down once and for all came the next day. I was down in the spring filling a couple of five-gallon jugs with drinking and cooking water. Suddenly, the air around me was broken by a *snap, snap*! It was the sound bullets make when passing by, before a gun's report when you're at the receiving end. These two bullets passed by close to my head. It was followed the next instant by the reports of .22 rifles shots. Surprisingly, I didn't flinch, or dive to the mossy spring for cover. I showed no fear. I was fed up with Sam Connor.

I knew it was Sam shooting bullets past my head to scare me. How did I know that it was Sam that was shooting past my head? Because he was the only one that had a semi-automatic .22 rifle, and a .22 bolt-action rifle could never spit out bullets as fast as a semi-auto. If he had wanted to kill me, I would have been dead. Instead, I waited for him to come closer, knowing all the while he would not even dare, but just in case, I was ready.

This spring area comprised of short waist-high willow, and he could plainly see me crouched over collecting water.

Willows

I continued to fill the five-gallon water jug. I had no gun, but I did have my hunting knife. Carefully, I unsnapped the knife case and waited. I am military trained for the art of hand-to-hand combat. I know how to disarm my capture, by taunting him to get close before I take his rifle, gaining control of the situation.

I could hear someone approaching stealthily through the undergrowth. Keeping alert, I focused my eyes and had my ears open, one hand on my knife; I waited.

Surprisingly, off to my side, on high ground near the spring, I saw Larry approaching with my big game rifle in his hands. "Boy, I sure am glad to see you, Larry!" Larry said.

"Boy, am I ever so glad to see you too, and alive at that!"

Larry walked over to me and gave his report. "I was way up by the dugout, and I heard the .22. Shots are going off down here.

I expected to see Sam standing over your body when I got here. I would have killed him on the spot," Larry continued to tell me. "I was sure he had killed you."

I think he wanted to, but his shots missed me, passing close to my ears. I did not move or grovel or show any fear. I am sure that's how he expected me to react. If he were aiming to kill me, he easily could have. "Tomorrow, Larry, you can be my backup. I am going to throw his *ass* out of here."

During my time in the army as a leader, my company commanders all knew me as being able to get men into shape. I knew my men well and proved myself to them as being a fair boss. Sam was not much different, and I certainly have had to manage worse than him. It would be like old times; I would have him respecting me in no time; I would do this by showing him respect first.

*   *   *

The next day, we went to have it out with Sam at his rotting, meat-stinking camp. Sam was waiting for us. He was high up off the ground on what was going to be a platform for a cache, twelve feet high. That is where he had set his tent up to be safe from any bear.

He was brandishing his big game rifle at his side.

"Sam, come down here!"

Sam slowly climbed down with his rifle in hand.

I spoke first. All the while Larry held my 8mm Mauser army rifle while he was standing to my side.

"Sam, I think it best you get a ride out on the next plane, for your good. The Federal Bureau of Land Management (BLM) did not recognize your claim for one thing, the other thing is you're only getting yourself into deeper trouble. How can I help you?"

Sam replied, "Duane, you're right. I am not equipped to survive out here, nor do I have the money to buy the supplies needed for me to remain here."

I suggested that he could either work for me, and earn his room and board, or help the neighbors. Until we found a way back to town, he would have to work here—for food. Once he was back in

45

Fairbanks, he could look for a job; he needed to work for money. That was the only way he was going to be able to recover from what he lost in his failed attempt at homesteading. In the meantime, once he got to the city, he could live in a homeless shelter, and go forward from there. If it had been the winter season when he went back to town, the job opportunities would be even less. His best time to recoup was now, but not out here in the wilderness.

"I have not only heard about people going through a story similar to yours, Sam. I have seen it myself. Why do you think out of the sixty-four land claims made in the Lake Minchumina Federal Land Settlement Area, only three remain, other than a few absentee landowners? At least, you tried, Sam. Don't be discouraged. Chalk it up as a learning experience and move on."

Sam had come to understand the realization that free land was not free.

"Sam, I heard an ad on the radio recently about a new fly-in-only lodge on Wien Lake. The lodge is in need of a helper, they are looking for an employee and are willing to help you catch a ride into town. The lodge is on the western shore, near the south end of the lake. You can walk there, it's on the map, and it's only about ten to eleven miles from here. You can see it from the top of the next hill to the north of here. Crossing ten miles in this North American jungle is no small task. I know you could make it in two days or less. I spent fifteen days crossing this treacherous land, and I want to prepare you for the challenges you will face. Think it over, and if you decide to do this, let us know. We have some grub you can bring with you, and some distress flares just in case." I felt it was my duty to warn him about what he might face in his quest to Wien Lake. I didn't want to discourage him; I was simply sharing the wisdom of my experiences.

With that, we went back to the dugout. Larry said to me, "You were a bit easy on him, Duane. I would have laid the law down on him."

"I did, Larry, I did. Only, it was a just law. Larry, I learned as a section chief in the army not to keep the flames of anger raging within a man when that man admits to his mistakes, but instead to help that man become your friend, and not break his spirit."

We knew Sam hadn't left his camp the next day when we heard him cough. Sound travels easily out here. Larry made a comment. "He's still here."

"Give it time, his brain is at work."

We both got a laugh out of that comment.

It wasn't until three nights later that we awoke to the trump-trump of heavy footsteps coming down the trail. We could hear footsteps made next to the dugout's wall. The door opened, and in popped Sam, like he had just won a prize for being gleefully victorious.

"Bet you can't guess what I just did," Sam said.

"No, I give up, what did you do?"

"I just came back from the lodge on Wien Lake."

"Why didn't you tell us that you were leaving? We could have taken care of your dogs until you came back."

"A plane is coming tomorrow at noon to pick me up. He's coming to the big round lake, not the one you use." He went on to tell us all about the hike he had just made.

Sam was excited, to say the least. Larry and I were in a daze. Sam asked me, "Duane, would you help me carry what we can to the lake tomorrow? Anything I leave behind is yours."

"What about the dogs?" I asked.

"Can they stay with you guys?"

"Yes, I guess so," I said.

"Okay, Sam, we need to get an early start. There is no easy trail to that lake, and it's a real jungle in places, including a creek to cross."

That night, Sam had the things by my door that we would be carrying to the lake the following day. "You best sleep here tonight since your tent is in that pile."

"Thanks, Duane."

Morning came, and Larry fixed a mess of pancakes for us. Off we went to my Honda, with the trailer full of gear. We went as far as the Frenchman's cabin. From there, we had about a one-and-a-half-mile walk with heavy packs. One and a half miles is not long on an open road, but this was not even, or open ground. It was made up of thick black spruce, marshes, and a creek we would have to negotiate to cross safely it.

We made it over the treacherous creek. We were nearing the shore of the lake; there were about a one hundred yards to go when the plane flew overhead. Our bad luck, we were in the coverage of trees, instead of out in the open where the pilot could easily spot us.

"It sees us."

"No, Sam, he is just flying overhead by chance. The pilot did not see us."

"Yes, it did," Sam insisted.

"No, he did not. Quick, drop your pack and run into the shallow lake, make like a duck, flap your wings."

The plane was on its third pass overhead, and Sam made no moves to get to the lake. He was standing there, still arguing that the pilot had seen us. On that third flyby, I raised Sam's .30-06 to my shoulder, took aim to the left of the plane, and as it were in the climbing mode to leave, *boom*! I fired to signal the pilot, hoping he would hear the blast past his left side, under the wing. I was careful not to hit the plane.

T. Lake

The float plane dropped, diving like a rock. The pilot had heard the *boom*. The pilot landed his plane and waited, standing on a float looking around. Sam was wading out knee-deep toward the plane, looking like General MacArthur proudly wading to the beach, but in Sam's case, to the float plane.

"I was headed to the barn leaving. If you hadn't fired that shot, I wouldn't be here."

Sam said to the pilot, "Bet you don't know what I did?" (Sam was referring to the cross-country walk he took to the fly-in lodge alone, needlessly risking his life.)

The pilot said, "Yes, I do. That was dumb." The pilot, whom I had never met, helped Sam get his stuff on the plane, and off they went.

Now for the rest of that air rescue story: Larry had been watching the plane from far away up at my house site. Viewing only the plane in the air, not us or the lake, Larry had seen the plane in a power climb, then saw it fall from the sky, dropping below the tree line out of sight. That happened at the same time he heard the *ker-boom*!

"*Damn*! Duane just shot the plane down!"

It was not until I got back up to Larry, telling him, no, I had not shot the plane down, did Larry relax. That then leaves us the dogs of Sam Connor's of which, in the days to follow, Dennis Hannan came and took them to be theirs.

At this point, I've wasted enough of my life discussing the likes of Sam Connor. I think it best to get this episode over and done. The idea of that moocher bothers me still, as it did back then.

Now on to the more important stuff, the work Larry and I were doing to improve my claim.

CHAPTER 5

Suzie Is Killed

Larry's hunting dog, Suzie, was his friend and companion. Larry had told me she was the best damn duck retriever in Minnesota. He loved his dog, and every chance they had, they hunted together. We never went hungry because there were always upland birds to eat thanks to Suzie. Suzie was an excellent pointer and retriever.

Bears, on the other hand, would prove to be her undoing. Suzie never experienced a bear in Minnesota. Here, she could sense their power whenever confronting a bear but failed to learn in time on how quickly a bear could wheel about on one foot when attacked from behind.

Suzie would come from behind to nip the bear on its hind legs when running off a bear. Suzie had a natural distaste for bears and would run them off whenever they were seen or heard. The bears would keep coming back, I think just to torment Suzie.

One day, Larry was headed back to the dugout where Suzie stood guard. As Larry approached closer to the dugout, he realized there was a scene of commotion. He could barely make out what he was seeing, but he could clearly hear Suzie entangled with a bear. He ran as fast as he could toward the fighting, just in time to see Suzie running a bear off uphill. That was the worst encounter Larry had seen between Suzie and a bear.

The battle area by the dugout had signs of the scuffle and some traces of blood on the ground. Suzie did not come back that day as she had in the previous encounters. Larry walked up the ridge and on past our dugout, calling Suzie to come back. There was no sound or sign of either the bear or Suzie. Larry had walked up the trail a considerable distance before he came back to the dugout.

As Larry was backtracking and close to the dugout hillside, he found one of Suzie's large teeth. It became very apparent that Suzie had been in a real tough battle, she might not be able to come back, and it was a possibility never to find her. Wherever she was, she was probably hurting.

That night, we thought it best that we take turns being on guard by the door's window watching for either the bear or hopefully Suzie's return.

I was on watch during the three o'clock hour, when I heard slow creeping movements approaching the dugout. I wondered if it would be a bear or Suzie. Quietly, I switched the safety switch of the rifle to the fire position, for being this close, even a click sound could have alerted a bear. The next moment I could see it was Suzie. Clearly, she was hurting, looking like she was sneaking home to her dog dish and water bowl. I woke Larry. "Larry! Suzie's back." Larry went to her, to comfort her, welcoming her back. It was obvious to see by Suzie's body language that she was not happy and was beaten badly to within an inch of her life. Her tail was down, and her belly dropped to the ground. Suzie was not in a cheery mode.

After taking some time of eating and drinking, slowly, Larry went about feeling her body for broken bones. Suzie twinged when Larry touched her left side. "Yup, she has broken ribs and a swollen jaw."

"Have her come inside, Larry. I am making a soft pad for her."

Suzie was shaking as she made her way to the inside. It took a long while for her to find a comfortable position, but finally, she fell to sleep. She did not have any scratches but had been tossed around by that bear.

Morning came and with it the need for Suzie to go out and use the bathroom. It was not a fun trip for her to go outside; clearly she was in a lot of pain.

"Larry, you stay here with her today. I can saw up the planks for decking the lake dock we're building. (The lake was three and a half miles away). I will be gone most of the day, so I will pack a lunch and bring with me the handheld CB. I will call you every once in a while, and again before I head back up."

Midday, I called Larry. "Larry! Got your ears on?"

In a few moments, Larry replied, "Bad news, Duane. Suzie is dead. She went to sleep and did not wake up."

"Oh, I'm sorry, Larry. I will be right up, but first, I will make her a head marker, out of white spruce lumber."

I asked Larry when I came back to the dugout, "Where do you want to her to rest in peace?" That was not a hard choice to make for him because it was well-known to Larry the location Suzie frequently liked to be. That was a place overlooking the southern valley views. Suzie had a favorite place up the hill's ridge from the dugout. It was on a knoll that she could overlook the countryside to the south and down at the dugout.

Suzie's head marker

Larry talked about the many hunting experiences they had taken the time to cover slowly her, taking breaks, resting on his shovel in between his memories told, to me and on camera. He in time buried her there, placing the head wood marker with a few words carved in, and then I gave it a preservative stain coating.

Suzie's death took a toll on Larry; they had been a team.

CHAPTER 6

Little People

The Hairy Ones, Commonly Known as Bigfoot
June 13

I awoke as usual but unaware that this day would prove to be one I shall never forget—a life-altering day forever burned in my memory bank. That was the day I would realize the wilderness is home to living in solitude, unusual beings.

I decided today I would hop on my ATV and drive up on the ridge trail. I wanted to search for the last few straightest of the black spruce trees we would need for making the smokehouse logs. The smokehouse was going to be a small cabin structure. I didn't want to use the straight and majestic white spruce for anything but the log house I was planning on building. I had in mind to take all the white spruce I could find for miles around for my future home. The lesser crooked black spruce was good enough for a smaller building. For the log house plans, I had in mind would take all the white spruce I could find.

The construction of the smokehouse was coming along nicely, even with all the other projects we were busy working.

Beginning of smokehouse

Those projects included:

1. the building of the one-hundred-foot by four-foot dock at the lake,
2. hunting grouse for fresh meat
3. brushing clear my four property lines that had to be four feet wide, to sight a transit for surveying, this was a requirement to approved for the homestead,
4. to hauling water up the hill from the spring below,
5. the building of a shower house,
6. making a garden,
7. then the making of a hillside 1,500-gallon pond (the first pond) plumbed to keep our three 32-gallon water barrels full to use for immediate washing, and showering on demand.

These water barrels were placed high on the ridge above the dugout, to give us free flowing forty pounds per square inch water pressure.

Water barrels

I would be looking for a timber source uphill. That made good sense to me, for it would make for easier hauling, bringing the logs downhill for our projects. I didn't have to search very far when I came to a dense stand of black spruce. It was only about one thousand feet away from the dugout and near the narrow ridge trail.

I parked the ATV, holstered my Estwing hand ax, and cleared a drivable trail to the stand of spruce, which was off to the east side of my main trail. All I wanted to do today was locate the straightest trees of the size I needed. I was going to blaze them and trim the branches to make them safely accessible for falling. I would return the following day to fall and pull them out to the main trail.

This dense stand of black spruce is up on a slight three-foot raised permafrost wet flat plateau, which sloped slightly down to the east. This flat ground would make for easy collecting of the logs. Only new smaller brush growth was in this dark stand of timber; there were no old deadfalls to worry about for negotiating my ATV.

There were several perfect trees in this thick stand, by the trees having grown close together made for straight trees. I would have a readily stand of trees to pick from, and fairly close to the exit haul trail that I had cleared. I'm well-known for having a pocket notebook on me. In this case, I used it for keeping track of the number of trees I had been blazing.

The exit trail was about 150 feet long, running southwest to the main ridge trail.

There was a slight wind from my left, coming out of the northwest. However, in this dense grove, only the treetops were moving. I was busily blazing the trees that I would be falling and trimming their lower branches off for tomorrow's falling. In selecting a tree, I had to look up at a tree first from one way, and then again from a quartering angle, to be sure it was a straight tree. I had blazed-marked about four trees when I started to get a sense of uneasiness, a stared at sort of feeling. At first, I thought nothing of it, but it did not go away. Instead, the feeling became stronger, more intense.

While I continued blazing trees, I shrugged off this feeling. After all, I was on a mission. I had no time for any distractions.

Finally, I couldn't ignore the feeling any longer. I thought to myself, *Okay! I give up. So I'm being watched.* But I wondered what it could be that was giving me these eerie feelings. I did not wish for whatever it was watching me, to know I was aware of its presence. I was curious and wondering to see what was watching me; would it be a wolf, a bear, moose, wolverine, fox, or what?

In my past, I hunted deer in Minnesota with a bow and arrow. I used this keen sense of "knowing that watched feeling" to my advantage. I would put the deer at ease by showing no reaction, letting it think it remained undiscovered. I would simply continue with whatever I had been doing.

For example, sometimes I would hunt from the forenoon until midafternoon. As I would progress with stealth near a game trail, on occasion a deer would be bedded down nearby the trail. As the sense of feeling watched came over me, I would make an effort to spot what was watching me, and most often it was a deer. If I hesitated in my movement forward, the deer would recognize that it was seen and bolted off into cover. Instead, I would continue walking, but at the same time locate the deer. I would draw back the bow, aim, and shoot, all in one fluid motion.

I would aim above it, where it would most likely be the instant it jumped to its feet. When I released the arrow, the deer would spring up with lightning speed upon hearing the bowstrings thump, while the arrow was now in flight. The deer often sprang right into the arrow's flight path, and I would have my deer. If instead had I loosed the arrow at the deer's heart while it was lying down, the deer would have been missed by feet, and the arrow stuck in the bed of the deer.

One time in the early hour of predawn light, while walking toward my deer stand, I had this sense of feeling watched. I carefully stepped off the path to the side, stepping behind a tree, and got ready to shoot. Within a few moments, a big buck that had been curiously following me appeared, and I then had my trophy deer. So I was very familiar with the watched feeling.

On this day, while I was in the stand of black spruce, I had no weapon with me other than my hand ax and hunting knife. I hadn't set out with the intent of killing anything; I was only there to select and mark the trees for logging. While standing in the shade of the trees, the watched feeling was becoming even more intense than I had experienced before. I heard a loud *snap*! It had to have been a large stick broken. Only an animal of considerable size could have caused that big of a sound. There was only the one quick sound, so I was unable to pinpoint the location, only that the sound was not very far from my right side.

I was still in the mode of selecting trees, but this time, I unclasped my razor-sharp hunting knife. I wanted to be able to draw it out fast if I should need it for close combat. I had sufficient training in killing with a knife, but I would far and above prefer using a rifle or handgun. I adjusted my grip on my hand ax to make sure it was extra tight and secure. The eminent danger I felt at that point was akin to live or die. I wasn't scared but on high alert.

That time as I played unaware of whatever creature was watching me, I moved about pretending to select trees. I did a grid search, starting at my feet and worked out from them. I was identifying every leaf, twig, wildflower, stick, stump, blade of grass—seeing everything for what it was. Most hunters look for the whole animal as if to say hi, here I am, but no, I look for an eye, a leg, and an ear, any small part that is not a plant, but that of an animal. If it was a grizzly bear, I might have to defend myself. I knew not to run from a bear, which would be fatal. Walk away maybe, but never run, sometimes a scramble to climb a tall tree is needed.

An adult bear cannot climb a tree, but they can reach as high as fourteen feet. They will push and push on the tree rocking it back and forth trying to shake you out of it. If you never knew how to climb a tree before, you will quickly, without thinking, find yourself scrambling up that tree without any instruction.

Not only was I searching the forested ground, but up off the ground, high up in the trees too, as a young bear has no problem climbing a tree. A cub in a tree would mean there was a momma bear close by in most cases, and that would be big trouble.

Nothing scares me, as long as I am in control, but being armed with only an ax would not give me a lot of control if I was facing a mad mamma grizzly. I decided then the safest choice would be for me to withdraw from this forest, exit the trail back to my ATV, and head down to the dugout, calling it a day.

I'm out of here. Bye, bye!

I remained on full alert while walking slow and deliberate to the beginning of my exit trail.

In this exit area, no green spruces were growing. It was mainly large white birch, spaced from eight to twenty feet apart. It was mostly open and viewable old-growth birch forest.

I began to think ahead about what steps I would need to take to make the quickest exit. Turning the ATV on was not as simple a matter as just turning the key.

First, I would need to turn the key to the on position. Then the shifting lever had to be in neutral. The slide switch switched in the run position. Then press the start button to start.

From time to time in the past, I have momentarily forgotten this procedure, when I have been in a hurry. A mistake like that now could prove very costly. I don't want to find myself pausing to think, *Okay, what do I do next?*

I was nervous but prepared for anything or most anything.

I was halfway back down my exit trail, when suddenly, some eighty feet to my left, I saw the animal that I could only assume had been watching me while back in that dark, dense spruce forest. It was exiting the spruce forest too. Apparently it had lost sight of me and was walking away from that dark, dense, forested area as well.

It was obvious it did not know where I was, but it was unknowingly paralleling me.

Instantly I froze, standing still in place. By chance, I happened to be close to a large birch tree inches to my left side, partially concealing me and blending me in. The front part of my body was ahead of this tree, in full view. I slowed down my heavy breathing so I could not hear it. Slowing down my breathing would keep my shirt from moving. I looked down at my chest to see my heart beating rapidly. I tried to pull back my chest within my shirt so that the racing heartbeat movements would not show.

What had shocked me into reacting in this manner was because I was watching a being I had never seen before. It was walking on two long legs, swinging its notably long arms with open cupped hands, taking long steps as it walked swiftly. I could see that anatomically it was a male being. It was choosing the placement of his steps, not making a sound. It was not turning its head from side to side to look about but was only looking forward as it walked.

Walking Hairy One

(Groundcover was of one-foot thick moss with a mix of debris.)

It appeared to be a naked man with long black hair covering most of the body like that of a black bear, but unlike the hair on a bear, his hair was twice as long. A male, and not female, as it had no breasts. He was about six feet tall. His profile was an all-muscular being. He had large, pronounced eyebrows. His nose was flat, smooshed into his face. Very noticeable was that he had no rounding of the forehead like humans.

Up immediately from his large, pronounced eyebrows, his bald head sharply angled high to the back of the head, at a forty-five-degree angle. His sharply sloping bald head came to a wide ridge point, and several inches higher than a human's head. At the top ridgeline of his head, he had long hair covering, and it dropped off straight down in line with his back.

His pointed cranial mass is not configured round like that of a human. He certainly could not have had the same size brain mass of a human.

From the top of his pointed forehead, long hair hung straight down his back, showing no back curvature, other than being tipped forward slightly as he walked. Long hair concealed his apparently short neck and covered his rounded shoulders. Most of his short but wide neck wasn't visible, only the front of it. I could just make out under his hair that he had cauliflower ears, not like humans, but the only nubbin-shaped flesh for ears.

His hands had five digits each, four fingers, and a thumb. The back of his hands and fingers covered with a shorter thin hair than that covering the rest of his body. His face, forehead, and palms were hairless; his skin was a grayish chalk black color. His fingernails were much like my own; only his were black. His arms were much longer in proportion than an average human's; they hung all of four inches lower than mine when they were swing at his sides. His lips were fat, big lips. He showed no teeth. His mouth closed. He also had a large chin and a pronounced jawbone structure.

He began to turn toward me, exposing his thick hairy muscular chest, giving me a frontal view.

One face-to-face

When he was facing me, I saw that his face was mostly hairless; his skin wasn't a true cold black shade but a more grayish tone. His nose was flat and wide; it looked pressed into his face, with no bridge. His large nostrils flared. His eyes were large, a deep black, and most impressionable bright. From the rear top of his head, the sides on down over his shoulders, his straight hair covered him like that of a haystack. No hair on his forehead, but on the side covering his ears and cheeks.

I am old enough to remember the cartoon character, Denny the Dimwit. This creature's pointy head reminded me of him, except for the face. The face was like the face of an ape, with wide set eyes.

I could not see any male parts between his thick hairy legs, just thinner hair where his legs joined his torso. His entire body covered two-inch black straight hair, which covered on down to the upper part of his feet. The hair at his ankles was longer than the rest of his hair. It resembled, but shorter, the flared cuffs of hair the Clydesdale horses have their hooves; only it was over humanlike feet. He walked right past me, coming within thirty feet between us. I got a good view of his backside and noticed there was no tail. If it had been a black bear, there would have been a short tail. He crossed over the main trail, coming within a few feet from the front of my ATV, and then he continued beyond into the thick woods.

From the first time I laid eyes on him and now even after he had disappeared in the thickness of the dark woods, I remained motionless all this time, and while I was watching him, I first would move my eye then my head very slowly. He was sneaking way and wanted nothing to do with me. I must have had nerves of steel, for it was not until he had passed me, and well out of view nor could he have heard any sound of me. Did I again begin to move slowly and yet quietly? Also, it should be known that all the while I did not smell him as the steady genital wind was from me to him.

When I got on the ATV, I made no mistakes in the starting procedure and hastily drove on down the ridge. It was not until after I become downwind of the hairy one did I smell the remnants of a powerful god-awful stink.

All in all, he looked like a very hairy human, only with a gray gorilla face, and exceptionally long arms and legs. Otherwise, he looked to be a middle-aged adult. He was not the monster, as some people would make him out to be. He wasn't a giant but was definitely in shape, like an athlete. There was no flab or bulging on his stomach; he was very muscular.

I was not the first to have such an encounter in this region; the natives in Alaska call these hominid beings Little People, and they never have described them to me as I do not think many have seen them. This one I saw was not little, so I think the name Little People came from the ones that are the most likely seen. The young teenagers in size, being they would be the curious foolish ones, thus the name Little People.

Also, it is my opinion that they live out their winter months as the semi-hibernating grizzly bears do.

Within the next few months, I was never alone. The Hairy Ones, I come to call them, were always around watching me night and day. Larry had left right after the first sighting that I had and was backing home in Minnesota. During Larry's absence, I had other encounters, of which I write about further on in this book.

During my time alone, I learned that the Hairy Ones are highly intelligent social animals that travel together, or otherwise keep in contact, but in solitude, unlike the bear, in that they keep far from the humankind. Except in my case, where I had moved in on their land. The black bears are true hibernators and sleep until spring. But like a grizzly bear that get up from their dens off, and on during the winter when the temperatures are warming.

The Little People I suspect, too, most likely semi-hibernate. I reasoned this because of one den sinkhole cave I had explored and finding various wild dry food items being stored on laid-out racks of sticks above the cave's floor, or in the collection stage, but no tools, other than neatly put together nests. I have to conclude that they are harvesters of berries, mushrooms, roots, and store them for the winters conveniently inside their dens, or caves, much like beavers and squirrels store their winter food.

To kill a member of this race of Little People, whom I call the Hairy Ones, would be murder. They are, in my humble opinion, perhaps a relative of the human race, or midway between the gorilla, and human, the living missing link. Mainly because I know the consensus is that the chimpanzees have the closest genetic link to humans. But what I have seen far and away resembled the gray gorilla more than a chimp. I have found they mean no harm. I have my reasons for coming to these conclusions, which I will be covering in this book.

During my first sighting, I wanted no part of introducing myself. After all, this being was not a stranger that one would meet on a sidewalk but was a shockingly being, all tough humanlike. My reaction was to disappear to hide. For certain I was not going to say "Boo!" In hindsight, I should have made our acquaintance and had a sit-down conversation.

I let the hairy one go off into the woods out of sight for a long period before I began to breathe normally with heavy breathing of relaxation. My breathing was more like gulping air. I had to force myself not to hyperventilate. It was then after well past me that I shook like a leaf in a churning windstorm. My knees were knocking against each other like two hammers beating their heads bouncing. Now my heart was racing too.

Why now? I asked myself. *Why am I shaken up?* But I knew why I was trained to be a killer. To kill takes total concentration, a massive dose of adrenaline. I had no time to think or dwell but to remain unnoticed and still, all the while the creature had first come into view then walked by me. I was intent on doing my job, not to kill this time, but to have my brain locked in record mode.

What was happening now was my body was released, to recover, letting me start the ATV with no problem and drive on down, not once looking back over my shoulder. It was more important to keep my eye on the road to drive down to the dugout and Larry.

When I arrived alongside the dugout, Larry was splitting up cooking wood. We just nodded to each other, signifying hello. Larry continued with splitting wood for the cooking. I went inside to lie down for a bit of rest and contemplate of the encounter I just had. It was a short time later that Larry came in and began to fix supper. He said nothing, not even asking me what I found for logs up in the woods.

For that matter, I was not talking to Larry either, which was not normal.

Larry was preparing some hot dish. During this time, I was pondering whether or not I should tell Larry of what he had only before had read in a monster book or seen in a movie. To tell him about the incredible thing that I had just witnessed would not be easy, but he needed to know the same.

The food was dished up and on the table; Larry sat down and was ready to chow down. I, however, was slow to be seated. The reason I remained standing was that the table was small, and Larry's reaction could be explosive. I did not know quite what to expect his reaction to be. It would be safer for me to stay standing while I told him. I was curious how Larry would respond. Would he think he had a madman on his hands? How could I put his mind at ease, after I revealed my improbable encounter?

I was the first to break the silence. "Before I sit down, Larry, I have something to tell you."

That was all I said, and before I could get anything else out, Larry interrupted me with, "What, you too?"

I could clearly see that Larry was a bundle of nerves at this point. Up until now, I was only thinking of myself and had not noticed anything out of usual about Larry, other than the incredibly loud silence between us. It was highly unusual for Larry to be quiet, not saying a word.

"Okay, Larry, you go first."

Larry pushed himself back from the small table to the wall and looked up at me shaking his head from side to side slowly.

"Well, you saw me at the woodpile making kindling and cooking wood when you drove back down. I was working on that woodpile most of the day. I knew you were up in the spruce thicket marking trees. I was doing fine until things got creepy. I could feel I was being watched, even though I could not see what it was, just that it was from something up the hill. That feeling did not go away, until just before you came back."

Larry went on to tell me, "That was only half of it. There was an awful bad stink that I haven't *ever* smelled before in my life. I went in and got the big game rifle, came back out, and it still was there watching me, and it stank badly. It was nearby, but I could not see anything."

Larry then asked me, "What happened to you? Did you see it? Like I said, when you drove back it was gone."

I recounted to Larry the events that transpired while I was up in the grove of trees, a short distance from where Larry was.

We both were puzzled over how to describe the stink for days. Together, we ascertained the description of that bad stink. It was like the smell of a rotten pot of urine, left fermenting for a month in a child's warm bedroom closet. We agreed without a doubt that this describes the stink perfectly.

That sighting would not be my last, however, and it prompted me to have my movie camera always sitting at the table or my side whenever possible.

Larry was cleaning up after we are super, and I went down to the smokehouse to peel some logs. While I was peeling for some odd reason, I happen to look up the hillside, and there on the top of the ridge right in the open was one of those humanlike young men sitting on his legs watching me work. I had no gun or camera. I had no intent to shoot him, but I dearly wished I had my camcorder.

Sitting Hairy One

I tried not to let him know I saw him, so I continued working but eased my eye his way. I know I could not sit the way he was and be comfortable. He was sitting on his heels broadside but facing me. His arms were resting on his legs forward. I could see that his face showed no fear but only was studying me, like he might be wondering, *What the heck is he doing and for what?*

I looked down at my work then looked back up, and he was gone. All I know my brain has a permanent freeze frame picture embedded in it. Next time I will introduce myself because I felt comfortable and would like to know more of his kind.

The Hairy One

My personal sighting and description of what I saw the summer of 1987 by my home on Ose Mountain, Alaska, that an artist friend of mine, Kris Hartung, followed, sketching these three colored sketches.

That might be the same elusive animal in Alaska referred to as the Little People.

The first painting sketch is of the head and face. The face to me looks much like that of an ape.

1. The nose is flat pressed into the face.
2. The nostrils flared.
3. The smooth skin color is gray to black.
4. The eyes are large, round, wide, spaced apart, and shiny dark. I suspect they're larger to take in light to see in the dark. (Eyes are similar to that of an ape but spaced wider apart.)
5. The lips are fat, huge like blubber lips (like those of some people).
6. The eyelashes are long.
7. The eyebrows are haired pronounced thick and heavy bulging.
8. From the eyebrows, the head immediately slopes at a forty-five-degree angle to the top of the high head. The face and sloping head surfaces are hairless (bald).
   (This sloping head with no rounding off of a forehead is one of the unique features of this being.)
9. At the very top of the bald slope head, yet still wide at the top, the long black hair begins. Straight long black hair is slick, not scruffy or frizzy, but long hair extending straight down the back, and the sides to cover the shoulders, looking like a black-haired (hay) stack.
10. This head of hair covers the shoulders and its ears. I could barely make out the ears. They appeared to be extended nubbins just under the hair like cauliflower ear that of a boxer (sportsmen boxer). Ears are not like that of a human.
11. Below under the fat lips, the broad chin was rounding but was covered by hair, not a beard per se, but body hair. The frontal view was the only indication of a neck.
12. Because of the hair-covered head, there appeared to be no neck, and that might be as if there was a neck but was not very long.
13. Jaws were pronounced, outlined by his hair.

The Head and Chest or Torso Sketch

1. The chest was very muscular with super thick hair, but I could ascertain that it had no breasts. This being was a male. (Apes have no hair on their chests.) This guy had body hair everywhere except on his face and the palms of his hands.
2. The shoulders were rounding (not square). Head hair was covering the shoulders. Head hair was noticeable longer than the two-inch body hairs, but straight, not like a wild trapper of long, unkempt hair or like mine when not combed or trimmed.
3. Note: Apes also have short necks.
4. Arms were covered with two-inch hair; dangling hair ends at the elbows.
5. Waistline or belly: this guy was in shape, but no a sign of a belly. No flab whatsoever!
6. Broad of girth, but not overweight for its size.

Painting Sketch of the Full Body while in Stride

1. Six feet tall within an inch or two.
2. Arms were four inches longer than a human's arm.
3. Note: The four-inch longer arms impressed me and very much noticed. (Apes have long arms too.)
4. Arm hair was long until just before the hands, and then it was shorter.
5. The back sides of the hands were hairy but short, bristly like almost normal.
6. Hands were like that of humans, five fingers. He walked with his hands semi-open, not clinched. Arms were swinging as he walked briskly to me, and then on past me. Again, his palm skin was gray to black.
7. Fingernails, not claws. Also, gray to black in color.
8. Legs strong, no fat flabbiness, long hair, of normal length.

9. As he walked, he leaned forward just a bit as expected when walking.
10. The long hair top of his feet fluffed outwardly from the ankles like the hair on some breeds of horses that conceal their hooves.
11. There was enough hair to cover his privates, but there was some yellowing of the hair in that area.
12. Another sketch should be of him fully on his legs squatting as he watched me working from above on the hillside. Heels under his butt cheeks.

The third painting sketch of him, or a friend of his, is as I seen him in the squatting position while watching me.

Thank you, Kris Hartung, for following my description of what I saw in 1987, and by working together over the internet from my Alaskan wilderness home, Ose Mountain, to your home in Minneapolis, Minnesota.

CHAPTER 7

The World without Communication

The world without communications or human interaction can be a lonely world, especially for those who have adapted to the ease of social access today's technology makes possible. A person will realize the loneliness of isolation once they have entered the remote wilderness world. The mindset in this environment of no communication and isolation it creates varies between people. Not hearing the sounds generated by people and lacking the touch of another human being isn't easy for some to adapt.

Some people have no desire to seek out the true wilderness, but for many it's a dream. Being away from society, all alone with only nature for companionship, is a mentally healthy experience. Being alone gives one time to search their soul, time to reflect on their past and present, and to ponder their future.

Depends on the length of time that one, even two people, set for themselves to be alone is their test. That time length and severity of isolation can range from a weekend retreat with some friends to going out on one's own into the wild for months, or even years. Some people adjust well while others go bonkers, talking to themselves or having imaginary friends. When a person has endured isolation for a significant period and get the opportunity to talk to another person or people, the communication eventually flows fluidly, a nonstop chatter built up over time.

Experience has always been my best teacher, and I have been my experiment of being alone. Eventually when with people, again I would realize I had a sudden attack of diarrhea of the tongue and clamp my mouth closed. That is common for more than those that seek out alone time in the wilderness; it happens to people in retirement homes as well. The elderly put into retirement communities are rarely visited by their family or friends, except during holidays and important events. That leaves a significant amount of time and often isolated.

Keep that in mind the next time you are about to drive on by someone's home that may be living alone. Stop in to say hello, and ask if they need anything. It need not be an occasion or event, but anytime. I urge everyone to find the time to earn a treasured moment with someone who is lonely. It doesn't have to be with someone you know, but it is a chance to make someone feel cared for, who otherwise may feel abandoned.

Each person has a story to tell, knowledge to be passed on, and an opportunity to share a friendship. That is something I have spent much time doing and will continue to do. Whether it is in person, a written letter, a phone call, or even over the computer, there are many ways to reach out and have a positive impact.

There had been a time or two when I just had to get away for a while, for the busy fast world seemed to be crushing me. That happened to me while I lived in Minnesota, on the Ose farm, located north of Echo, as well as when I lived in Wood Lake. I would often go by myself to the Rock, my alone space—a fishing hole I would visit to escape the clutter of life's situations, a place to meditate and contemplate. In time, I would return to the world of people, with a renewed outlook, and ready to face reality anew, with a stronger handle on the tasks at hand.

If I had a dollar for every time I've heard from a casual camper, "This is the life. I could live like this forever," I would be a rich man. In reality, most could not last a week without the comforts of technology and without human contact.

A person doesn't have to be alone, to feel alone. It can be even more frightening feeling isolated but being surrounded by people. This odd feeling can happen by the uncomfortable feeling of not fitting in and the mind is in another place far removed from the physical reality.

Loneliness can occur anywhere anytime, which I can relate to as once myself having been a soldier remotely located in the demilitarized zone in South Korea surrounded by one hundred other fellow soldiers at Christmas. My mind was in two places at that time—one was thinking of being with Geri T., my Bronx, New York, girlfriend, two was my job at hand. I overcame that feeling knowing my men looked to me for leadership.

Larry Brau, his dog Suzie, and I lived and developed my homestead together well, but we were on the fringe of total isolation, only having a job to do and each other for companionship. It was Larry's first time living remote for an extended period. I, on the other hand, had done this often before, so conditioned in knowing how to adapt to the limited contact.

We had our close friends and family in Minnesota who sent messages to read to us by the station readers on air over the radio station KJNP Trapline Chatter AM 1170, located in North Pole, Alaska. That community is twelve miles south of Fairbanks. This radio station is a religious station, and once each night at nine thirty, they have a special service to the people in the bush that have no other means of hearing from their friends and loved ones.

There are those who live remote, like Larry and I during that time. Then there are the seasonal people, the miners, trappers, and the ones who work on the river barges during the summer.

(This era of time, 1987, there were no cell phones, satellite phones, or satellite internet, but there was analog television having long range capabilities with the use of big long-range antennas, or simply known as rabbit ears, a small adjustable dual antenna on the TV set.)

It was several long weeks on Ose Mountain before anyone sent us a message. To be fair, it does take five days for the US Postal mail to reach KJNP, from the lower 48 states. (All states are so far away, we Alaskans use the terms "outside" or "the States.")

On the nights when we would tune in, only to learn we had no messages addressed to us, we would say to each other, "No one loves us anymore." When the letters for us did start to flow, there was no end. We became quite popular over the air, having letters that were read to us each night. Some of the letters were so long that they had to be read to us in parts.

The readers of KJNP rotated so that each night there was a different reader, and that presented a problem to us sometimes. When a letter read to us in parts, often the new on-air reader would reread what had been shared the previous night, instead of continuing with the unread portion. Apparently the letters were not marked well by the readers, or at all. There were lengthy letters not read to completion due to the limited airtime. The letters saved for us to pick up if we were in the town of North Pole.

Our ability to send out the letters we compiled was unpredictable and unreliable. It could be months before a plane would drop in. We had homesteader neighbors some eight miles away, and across two lakes, living on the shore of a third, with whom we would chat with at night on our citizen band (CB) radios. Oliver Cameron and the Hannans at this time were the only other ones out here. Communicating this way, we could keep each other posted as to when any of us had a plane due in so we could get the mail to Fairbanks. Larry and I would write longhand letters and record audio viewable letters on VHS tapes to be sent out. To have any mail sent out was never timely. One reason was the three and a half miles from the dugout to the mailbox on the dock. It could be months before mail would be picked up by a pilot that had another reason to be at the dock or the Hannans'.

Eventually, a plane would come, and our letters would be mailed out. When the news of Suzie's death by a bear reached back home, we received all kinds of sympathetic mail read to us over the air. No wonder, the bonding of a pet is family to most people; it is like being attached to the heart. This tragic loss felt by not only Larry but by Larry's father, who knew what Suzie meant to Larry.

Larry, naturally, was not feeling well after losing Suzie and came down with an ailment. Larry let his father know this and asked his dad to come and bring him back to Minnesota so that he could recover from his illness of most likely giardia. That is in the epilog portion of this book, pages from my diary Thursday, May 14.

CHAPTER 8

Federal Bureau of Land Management Approves My Homestead Claim

t was time for me to define and establish the property lines. I knew the lay of the immediate land around my homesite, and I had assessed the best way to make improvements, in regard to the location of my future home.

1. The house would have a southern drop away view.
2. I would have a garden, with a large lawn.
3. Higher up on my land, a rainwater holding dam, for gravity flowing water on demand.
4. I also had mapped out the best places for trails to access my property.

Because of my permanent disability and my earned disability fixed income awarded me, I had no choice but to file only for a five-acre home site, or give up my disability income by having to make and prove an income derived from an eighty-acre trade and manufacture site or a five-acre headquarters site.

My property lines for a home site needed to be measured to enclose five acres, to be laid out in a true north, south, west, and east directions rectangular in shape. The north-south lines would be 660 feet and the east-west lines to be 330 feet, establishing this perimeter enclosing my new land. This small piece of the Alaskan wilderness land that had spoken to me, in a hush of whispering wind saying "c-h-o-s-e me," and in turn my heart said "y-e-s."

I would have to make the alignments true north, south, west, and east with a simple handheld magnetic compass. Topographic maps for every section have on them a compass declaration indicating true north. I could then adjust my high-quality magnetic compass and know the correct degrees as to where true north is from the magnetic north on the earth's global map. As a former scoutmaster trained in map making, I was well-versed in the art of mapping the land.

These lanes have to be wide and close to perfect, to allow for errors. I made these needed cleared lanes four feet wide so the surveyors could use their transits to adjust, and set, marking the exact corners of my property to record accurately onto the map of Alaska.

I drove in the first property stake on the south west corner that I was certain about to include it in my property. Then by using the compass arrow that I had set, rested the compass on top of that first corner stake. Aimed the compass arrow, then fixed in my mind the spot on the ground the compass needle pointed to and drove a stake in on that point. I then went back to the corner stake, aimed the compass again, but this time, to see if the second stake was yet in line on the right spot. The second stake then placed, and I was right on course.

With the two stakes inline, it was easy to complete the first line by jumping ahead of the second stake, then by looking back aligning the two stakes and drove in a third, continuing with more wood stakes to keep the line on the course. After that, I proceeded to clear-cut the first line four feet wide, measured and drove in the second corner stake. By using this method, I proceeded to complete the next three lanes.

I used strong, stout, straight stakes that I had sawn from my previously milled lumber. To aid me, I used survivor's flagging in roughing out the next three lanes first due to the dense forest, bit by bit, and chainsawed the line as I measured my way to the ends of each, collimating on the first corner stake. The returning alignment was right on to the first stake. That was a wonder I must admit. Diligence and patience proved to save me time.

This land was a virgin jungle, thick with trees, undergrowth, sloping land with rolling ups and downs accurately measured. With a recently purchased surveyor's tape, this is an extra-long measuring tape. I kept this tape pulled tight all the while driving stakes at certain points straight in the lane until I completed all lanes to the corners, pounding in the important stakes. Surveying on a forested hillside was demanding, to say the least, not like that in an open, clear view flat prairie.

I paid close attention to keeping my alignments. I knew that in this job, haste would make waste. As it was, it took me two full days to make my four cut-cleared lanes and ended up being right on the first try. Of course, I checked at the end of the initial survive three more times to be sure. (Years later, the official land surveyor's found I was off on the final corner by six inches. It was the best measuring of land they had seen by a homesteader.)

My physical address is Kantishna Section 36, Range 20, and Township 8 Denali National Park, Alaska. Needed for voting and is on my voting card. The exact survey recorded in the Fairbank's Land Office.

On July 9, unannounced, a Cessna 185 with floats on flew over our heads bussing us five times, and then this plane headed toward the lake. Larry and I assumed it was the BLM coming in to inspect my claim to be approved or disapproved. Larry took the camcorder and took motion pictures of the plane while I hopped on my ATV. I drove as fast I dared down the three and a half miles of tree stump– stumbled trail, trying not to hit a standing tree or (making light of here) have one jump out at me on the way to greet the BLM team at the lake.

I arrived at the dock just as they had offloaded from the plane and were standing on the dock. The charter plane was Wrights Air Service of Fairbanks. I had recognized the plane when it flew over our heads at the dugout on its first pass as being the company plane from Wrights. On this plane were the young pilot and three employees from the Federal BLM Office, one of which was a woman. After a short introduction, we made our way up the hill to the dugout. Of course, the young lady rode with me on the ATV.

During the drive, I would drive on ahead to stop and wait for the others at different points of interest, but more so to give them a rest. At the first quarter of a mile, I stopped to show and tell them of the Frenchman's cabin. Then again at the half mile marker, I told them they were now in the Enchanted Forest, and why the name by explaining that whenever in this tall old growth forest, I had the feeling of being watched by whatever resided within it whenever I would pass through. But in time, I accepted the fact that I was never alone in these woods.

Frenchman's cabin

At the first mile marker, the trail was a straight uphill long cut made up of new trees from anywhere from two inches up to eight inches in diameter. I informed them I had named this section of trail Rifle Ally because this long straight lane was where I sighted in my rifles. Then next was Moose Lane, an area on level ground of newer short growth birch and aspen trees, which was a great foraging area for the moose. As we began the last uphill grade, the Golden Forest came into view. I had named it that because when Jeff Peterson and I first reached this section of the forest in 1986, it was early fall and the forest color was of gold.

Lastly, we turned right, eastward, through dense cover on each side of the trail approaching my domain, Ose Mountain. This land opened up to a page in a storybook. Nestled among huge timber of white birch, with towering white spruce trees with an ayah inspiring view, looking out over, and down at the mountains floor of five lakes with the warm sun on our faces.

This location has been untouched by wildfires for at least five hundred years due to the windless sheltered cove of this hill. This sheltered cove of hillside land I called the cupped hands of God. Wildfires have gone around this area, and so this was a reassurance to me that I seldom will have a fire in this location. I would in time trim and clean the grounds free of debris, the fuels that would feed a fire preventing a wildfire from burning this beautiful sheltered heaven on earth land.

I came to a stop on top a steep ridge; the woman and I dismounted off of the ATV. I turned to look at the boss of the Fairbanks district BLM land office, the pilot, and his office aid. At that moment, Larry and Sam came up from the dugout. We were all standing together when I said welcome to Ose Mountain.

The BLM boss in the Fairbanks District Office asked, "Where's your cabin, Duane?"

"Come on, I will show you."

They walked up to my side, and I pointed down at the moss lushes green-covered dugout that was on the lee side of this same ridge. Then we walked down to the dugout, to see the dugout with its outer walls made of home-sawed lumber each board lapped over the lower one to shed the rain.

Everyone gasped and looked in amassment. The boss wore a plaid black-and-white checkered shirt and a campaign hat or, as you might know, it is better as scoutmaster's green hat with a chin tie. The boss had his books and maps sticking out from his deep back pockets.

Moss covered dugout and the boss's papers in hip pocket

Larry opened the dugouts massive four-foot wide and insulated four-inch thick door with its wooden four-foot hinges. "Go on in," Larry said. "Anyone want tea, coffee, or a glass of Tang?"

We seated ourselves at the small table, on the edge of the lower bunk, and on empty five-gallon gasoline cans. Larry was a very good host, and no one went without a drink or became hungry. Us all enjoyed Larry's fresh made cookies.

The boss was a tall, slender man. As he looked about, he stood up and stretched his right arm and hand high above his head, then asked me, "What is the height of the ceiling? What are the dimensions?"

Larry said, "The measurements are 9½ feet high, and 9 feet by 11 feet. The walls are 6 inches thick and insulated with orca moss. On top, the log roof is 21 millimeters of poly sheeting on that is 8 inches of ground covering moss."

The boss with his 35 mm camera took a large number of photos while he looked around asked me additional questions. It was about then that Sam Connor spoke up and said, "You have to see my place too. It's just a ways over from here, follow me."

It was not long before the whole team came back from Sam's camp but without Sam. The boss asked for me to show him my cut and cleared property lines. He looked down the cuts, clearly seeing how well cleared the cuts were and confirmed the surveyors would have no problem.

Then while Larry and others went out to look the area over, the BLM boss, one of his office aids, and I stayed in to do some paperwork.

Question 1: "When did you move into the dugout?"

Answer: "Well, Jeff Peterson and I in 1986 lived in this while we built all this up around us and removed the soil within in stages. But officially, Jeff and I pounded the last nail November 10th of the last year 1986. Then this year, Larry and I have been living here since the 14th of April, and I will be living here to the 19th of September. That would meet my required of five continuous months of one year of living here in a habitable dwelling. As a veteran, that is my required time."

Question 2: "What dollar amount would you put on this dugout, Duane?"

Answer: "I had not given it a thought until you asked." I thought to myself of the materials, the chainsaws, the stove, chimney, not including the labor, then said, "Oh around $950."

"*What?*" the boss said with a gasp.

I repeated, "$950!"

The BLM boss said, "No way, I am filling in that space on the form for $10,000, no. Scratch that, I will make it $20,000. Duane, do you have any idea of what a one-room, unimproved, with no running water cabin cost in Alaska?"

I said, "No," and then I got educated.

"Duane, when you get into Fairbanks, drop in at my office. The paperwork will cost $10.00 plus $2.50 per acre, and since you have lived in this habitable dwelling dugout for the required amount of time, which I have highly approved of I may add. Your claim is approved, and since you're an army veteran, the surveying will be done as the scheduling can be arranged at no fee. Duane Ose, let me be the first to congratulate you on your success." After that we shook hands.

It was then I asked, "May I ask how Sam Connor's did?"

He looked at me as he laid out the big scroll of paper that had the sixty-four total claims marked on the map. He placed his pointer finger in a place that is two miles south with a code identifying the number on it for each name on a claim, and some east of my claim. "There that was where Sam claimed, not up here," the boss said. "I knew right away when he marked it on the map in my office that he had never physically been here because I knew it is all swamp land he had marked. Sam had only paper claimed, and doomed from the start, but I did ask him, are you sure? Without hesitation, he told me yes. I said nothing more to Sam." (Note: To paper claim only is not allowed.)

"Besides, he has done nothing in the way of proving up at this site here by you. I did not approve his claim."

I then said, "So Sam wasted all his time out here then."

The boss said, "No, he just had an experience many will never have. Sam is young. He will be wiser for this experience."

It was then time to head back to the plane, but not before more pictures were taken, and one of me in front of the dugout. It was not until later, I seen my photos attached to the walls of the boss's office in Fairbanks showing me as a successful homesteaders example.

The BLM district boss also went on and told us of the second area the Solana Federal Land opening area of thirty thousand acres near Tok Junction, southeast of Fairbanks near the Yukon Territory of Canada. While down there, he, the boss, carries a handgun for self-protection from the many harassing nearby road onlookers. The BLM company cars that are left parked on a pullout parking area off the highway are not safe from vandalism even if parked empty. So they need to be occupied by one person or driven away to return later to pick up the returning BLM inspecting team after they had done their inspecting of the claims of that land opening area.

That confirms my choice of this Lake Minchumina Federal Land Settlement, opening for sure. It might be super remote here but safer. To have a home anywhere in a rural area often gets broken into not by a bear but by drive-by thieves even in a town. Here I can kill and eat my vandals (bears) but then, too, bears have respect for nail boards (boards with nails to penetrate the feet of a bear), and the boarded covered doors and windows when no one is home.

On our walk, and drive back to the plane we all were visiting, Sam was talking the boss's ear off, asking questions, and telling him of his times here. At one point I overheard Sam ask the BLM district boss, "What about this trail Duane made?"

The bosses reply was quick and short. He said, "He had to get here, didn't he!"

At the plane, we exchanged our goodbyes, and I said come back to visit anytime. The pilot and the boss did come back a few times through the following years.

On our way back up to the dugout, the three of us Sam, Larry, and me, at some point on the trail, Sam asked me, "Did you get approved?"

"Yes, Sam, I was approved."

Sam came back and said, "Well I wasn't."

"Yes, Sam, I know."

CHAPTER 9

David Brau Arrives July 16

Larry and his dad had been exchanging letters ever since a bear killed Larry's dog Suzie. It was not easy for Larry to get mail out often or on a regular basis. But Larry's father had in one of his messages on the Trapline Chatter, asked what we would like to have him bring in when he came.

We both added a short list of answers to that question. I only asked for a watermelon and soda pop. Larry asked for fresh eggs and fruit. There may have been other things too, but for sure I was craving watermelon.

Then April 14, a letter read to us on Trapline Chatter was a phoned-in message from David Brau. He was on his way to Alaska from Jordon, Minnesota, telling us he would be arriving in Anchorage at 9:00 a.m. the 15th, Wednesday. He also said he'd be sending more messages later.

Note here: This was the time before the advent of cell phones, so to make a phone call, it had to be done on a house phone or from a payphone.

From this sudden message phoned in read to us on KJNP radio, we could tell he was on the move and most likely made that call from a Minneapolis Airport telephone booth. The phone call was short because David was being sure to catch the boarding gate for the flight to Anchorage. Plus long distance calls were short due to the costs and the change in one's pocket. Dave was defiantly on the fast track to Alaska.

Wednesday was just another work day until later when we would tune into messages at 9:30 p.m. for an update from David Brau.

This day, I began nailing the roof boards on the smokehouse. I had it three-fourths completed by 9:00 p.m. Larry worked at a seconded bridge on the trail. Where the bridge was needed was a steep washout. That washout was a dangerous nuisance to drive across, so he was transferring soil to fill it in.

Then came the message time on KJNP, but there was no message from David Brau. However, there was one from Oliver Cameron, who was in Fairbanks. Oliver had been in contact with Jill's father who lives in the state of Washington. Oliver informed us that Jill's father was coming to spend a month around the 6th of August, and Oliver, too, thought he'd be back at that time.

Then a CB call came in. "Ose Mountain, Ose Mountain, you got your ears on? This is Muskeg Momma over."

I came back and said, "Sure do, Muskeg Mamma, go ahead."

Now what happened next, I must explain. Whenever we did not want anyone else to hear us talk while on the CB radio, like the Wien Lake Lodge personnel some ten miles north of me, we had code words we would say. That was "Catch ya later," then we would switch over to channel 31 from our known normal channel. Jill had said, "Oh I forgot, I am still feeding the kids, catch ya later."

The use of the citizen band radio was almost daily; it was a real asset to us all. That would mean no walking or the checking of the time, the weather, and all the fuss of travel.

Thursday, July 16

Larry and I had just eaten breakfast when out of the northeast over the trees, we heard the sound of an airplane, and it was headed right for us. We ran outside, and soon we saw above the heavily forested canopy a Cessna 185 with floats. It was the plane from Wrights. Larry was ecstatic and said, "Bet chaw that's my dad." I turned to say something back to Larry, but he was gone, and already over the ridge running downhill the three and a half miles to the dock. The plane circled overhead three times. I had a few things to take care of, but a half hour later, I was on the ATV and headed down to the dock too.

Dave B. and pilot on dock

This flight, Wrights Air Service, was Bob, the owner himself, who had flown the plane bringing Dave Brau with not only his traveling luggage but a load of goodies. Store-bought goodies that we hadn't seen since April 18 when we had first arrived here. Dave brought in one dozen eggs, a bag of large juicy plump oranges, a very big watermelon, two paper grocery bags of sweet corn, box of tomatoes, can of Tang, four bags of potato chips of different flavors, and a six pack of ballpoint pens. Envelopes, more shampoo, and hair combs.

Bob took the mail I had brought down; as usual Bob was very cordial and easygoing. I thanked him for bringing out David Brau on such short notice. He said, "No problem, I just happened to be handy. My pilots had scheduled flights to do. Duane, when I send the plane out here the 22nd to pick Larry and Dave up, would you like me to bring a load of gasoline? You might as well, Duane. You can pay for it COD by check."

"Gee, that would be terrific thanks."

With that, the owner untied the plane from the dock, gave the plane a shove, hopped on a float, climbed in, started the engine, taxed away warming the plane's engine, drove the plane to the north end of the lake, turned the plane south into the wind, and powered up.

The plane gained forward speed making a wave until one float lifted above the water, then a seconded later, the last float was airborne.

The plane continued gaining speed, climbing, and away from the lake, turned right, then another hard right, and bussed over us, rocking its wings waving goodbye, headed in the direction of Fairbanks. The loud sound of the powerful plane's engine was echoing from shore to shore until the silence came upon us once again.

As the sound of the plane was fading, the mosquitoes were making their continuous, increasing humming tune. It was time to have David apply the mosquito repellent.

A person without repellent is a blood bank to be tapped until all the blood is gone. Just to hear those mosquitos is horrifying. But to lose the battle in fighting them off as they attacked David by the swarm of zillions adding more in strength by the minute would kill David by draining him dry of blood. The blood-thirsting mosquitoes were drilling not only the exposed skin but through his light clothing. Heaven forbid if any of us had to go to the bathroom without repellent. Mosquitoes in Alaska are the worst on earth. A person without repellent would first go mad, and some people have considered killing themselves. It has happened. Mosquitoes swarm, making one black cloud and follow a victim, like bees in attack mode.

It has been my experience the two best mosquito repellents are Ben's 100 DEET and musk oil. The other brands are short-lived and cheap. It is best to pay good money for long-lasting repellent. Also, I never apply these powerful products to the skin, but instead apply on only parts of the clothing, or on a fixed surface of a working area of the nearby surfaces. These two products do not need to be liberally applied but in small amounts here and there. The black cloud of swarming mosquitoes will disappear and will stay well clear, giving you peace and ease of mind. Always have more of this strong repellent close at hand. Think of it like this: a smart soldier never runs out of ammo.

"Good to see you, David. David, how did you get here so fast?"

David went on to tell us how the ball got rolling in catching a plane right off without even setting a schedule. "It was like this," David went on to say, "at the ticket counter, I purchased the ticket for a flight to Anchorage that was to disembark in fifteen minutes. I made a call to KJNP, ran to the boarding gate. (No security check in those days.) It was a direct flight. I arrived in Anchorage, and the airline had I scheduled for the next morning to fly to Fairbanks. I then looked at the flight departures on the flight scheduling board and seen a flight was nearly ready to go to Fairbanks. I asked if I could get on that one. A woman behind the counter said, 'Sure at gate 4, that way around the corner, sir.'

"Then in Fairbanks, I hailed a cab, went to Freddie's, shopped, hailed a cab, went to a motel, and in the morning called a cab to Wrights Air, now I am here. Sorry, I had no time to update you. Man!" David sighed. "It has been a long day. You're three hours behind Minnesota time."

David appeared to be tired too, compounded by being in a different time zone. David had a real case of *jet lag*.

"No warning was needed. That's great, David. I still cannot get over on how fast you made it here all the way up from Minnesota."

"Duane, you're long ways from town here. I flew over at least four rivers, hundreds of lakes, and seen total roadless wilderness, but the flight out to here was good."

"Well, David, the best time to be in a small plane is in the morning for the smoothest air. You timed that right."

We then loaded the trailer, and together we headed up the trail. I drove, and Larry and Dave walked.

The day couldn't have been nicer, clear full sun, and seeing father-son out ahead of me was a wonderful sight in seeing them conversing. From what I could tell, Larry was doing most of the talking in showing his dad everything on the walk and asking him a lot of questions about back home.

A dead spruce tree had fallen across the trail after we had come down to pick Dave up, so Larry chopped it and moved it off the trail while David watched. Having a tree fall blocking the trail was a normal thing, and so it was best to remove it instead of trying to go around it.

Fallen tree and removing rope on the sled

They came upon a homemade dog sled that Sam had made early on for his dogs to pull. Then had abandoned it, it was made very crudely all tied together by ropes, and it looked like it was used partly only once. Larry and his dad removed the rope lengths, saving those for me, and tossed the wood sled parts to the side of the trail.

Sam had no clue on how to tie knots. He had just tangled the ends of the rope until they seemed to hold, no two tangled knots were the same, and interestingly enough made them hard to untie as there was no rhyme or pattern to them.

Brauzier's Bridge

When we reached Brauzier's Bridge, so named that because Larry Brau had built it and had a carved into the wood a sign placed high above it, "Brauzier's Bridge."

It was something Larry had wanted to build, making his mark. This bridge bridged a wide, deep depression that crossed the trail saving a lot of trouble in crossing it.

We arrived at the dugout and unloaded the trailer. Larry showed his dad around the area to see the rainwater collection pond, the water barrels for washing, the shower house, and the outhouse. Later Larry made supper, pointing out to his dad the nightly routine, of our communications, and listening to Trapline Chatter. Eventually, we went to sleep.

Next morning, Friday, July 17, we had eggs with all the fixings. I had forgotten how fresh eggs tasted better than powdered eggs.

Me working on the smokehouse

Larry and his dad went exploring the countryside while I continued working on the smokehouse and the other daily things to do.

That night, Jill Hannan called to tell us they were planning on coming up at noon Sunday if the weather was nice.

Larry called me to the side, telling me he now dreaded in going out and was worried about me staying behind alone, knowing what encounters we had with the Little People that we had seen. I reassured him I would be fine and not to worry about me, that I would be seeing him late September. "Really, Larry, I am fine, you need to escort your dad now. Have a wonderful trip. You have been looking forward for this a long time."

It bothered Larry to be leaving me here alone, but I had no second thoughts or fears at all. I guess to some being alone would be a concern. But it would be only two more months, and I would be driving down the ALCAN to Minnesota, of which I was looking forward to that leisurely fall scenic drive in Canada, knowing the trees down south in the States would yet be green.

Saturday was a rainy day, but I still was able to get some things done while Larry and his dad enjoyed themselves.

Sunday morning, early at seven thirty, I got up and went for a long walk to the big creek to the west, letting Larry and David sleep in late. Today I put on my better dress-up fancy traveling clothes as we were having company, the Hannans, Denise, Jill, Shaun, and Stormy.

They arrived about twelve thirty. The walk to us here on Ose Mountain takes them three hours, that involves a muskeg trail, canoeing a creek, canoeing the length of the long lake, a trail to Levi Lake, then around it to my gradual incline trail. In total overall travel for the Hannans, it is no less than eight miles.

Larry had fixed up a delicious picnic with all the stuff made for a July get together. I even think it was the first time the boys had watermelon since they seldom got into town and had lived out here since they were born.

Picnic eating, David and Dennis visiting, boys, Jill, and me

Larry saw to it that there were no empty hands or empty mouths, as he was a fine host and chef. The rest of us engaged in conversations and the telling of stories. David and Denise talked in length of the financial times we are in, with the farmers having to get bigger, the small farms disappearing, and the land prices gaining in value. With being caught up in having to grow to pay for the existing loans, American farmers were in a vicious spending cycle during this time.

I gave the Hannans a grand tour of the workings, the house site, smokehouse, water system, showering house, spring, even a walk up to the top to view north, and study the route of a trail to Wien Lake, making it a joint effort. We gave it no thought of a grant or a fundraiser to finance this project, but do it with what we had. We were an example of a hardworking local government united in one common goal with no bickering or debate.

Then later I noticed Jill checking her watch, and it was time for the wonderful Hannan family to head back to their home. It had been a fun day for all.

The next day, Monday, there was a light rain, but I had work to do at the dock, so I spent the day adding forty-two feet of framing to the dock. It was a day for Larry and his dad to rest and look around on the hill. I arrived back to the dugout at 9:00 p.m. for a late supper, and more watermelon, after which Jill called using the CB radio to visit, saying goodbye to Larry and Dave.

Tuesday, July 21, the weather was cooling off with threatening rain. Larry and Dave decided to pack up and move down to the dock to be ready for the flight, in case of bad weather for them to be walking down tomorrow. That worked for me for I had lumber decking to nail down on the dock, so I had lots of help.

Dock shelter

Using the Frenchman's Cabin, Larry cooked up a beef stew supper, but instead of Larry and his dad sleeping in the cabin, they built a shelter of poly sheeting on the dock and spent the night there. I guess David knowing or fearing the cabin was a one-fourth mile away from the dock was trying to save time not having to rush to the plane when it landed. The plane was unscheduled as to the exact time of the day, but around noon it would be there, weather permitting. (Here in the wilderness, it's both hurry up and wait, with no exact times.)

I drove back to the dugout knowing the plane would not be there until I returned in the morning or later. I had a good night's sleep, and in fact, it was the first night to be alone since I had slept in the tent for two to three days last year in September. While Jeff Peterson was at the Frenchman's Cabin, when he and I first broke the trail up from the Frenchman's Cabin or what we called base camp, I remember telling Jeff at that time, "I am not going back down to base camp that I am here to stay. You, Jeff, can go back and forth hauling the supplies up."

Wednesday, July 22, the departure date for Larry and his dad. I drove down to the dock and arrived there before they got up; it was a drizzly, foggy, cool day. We suspected the plane was due to arrive at noon, but with this weather, it may not be this day. We would just have to wait.

Then at 2:24 p.m., we heard a droning engine sound from out of the northeast. It was the plane! "The plane!" Larry said. "Looks like this is it, time to say goodbye. Are you sure you're going to be alright, Duane?"

"I'll be fine, and thank you for all your help. I will see you in September. Go now, not to worry about me."

As promised by Bob, the owner, he sent out twenty gallons of gasoline in five-gallon sealed cans of which I wrote out a check to Wrights Air Service for $30. That was for the cans, and the gasoline contained in them.

D and L loading plane burls

I took camcorder VHS movies of them loading the plane and them of me. The pilot did not have room for all of Larry's wood burls for this flight, so he had to leave a good number behind, of which I stored under the lake's dock to later take them with me in September if I had room on the plane.

Soon they were up and off of the lake heading to Fairbanks. Tonight they would be flying directly to Minneapolis from Fairbanks and arriving at the Minneapolis Airport, Minnesota, ten hours later.

The day after Larry and David Brau flew to Fairbanks on to Minnesota, July 23, I began working, taking two days of cutting an extended trail through a black spruce forest to the lake's outlet from my dock. The one-hundred-foot dock only days prior was now complete.

CHAPTER 10

Building of the Eighty-Foot ATV Bridge

The idea of building a bridge came to me when I realized the effort the Hannans had to put forth to travel between us. The biggest hazard for them was the outlet of Levi Lake. That is the lake where my dock is and where my trail to Ose Mountain began.

The bridge

The outlet of this lake had a twenty-foot wide span of water, which ran for a long distance before it turned into a narrow and a mucky bottomless bog. The bog drained into another lake, the lake I call Talking Lake. Talking Lake has a wide overflowing drainage that is one mile long and empties into Long Lake.

In traveling around Levi Lake's outlet without getting wet, a fallen tree or wood debris had to be used at some narrow point. That was a dangerous task because the rotting stuff is bottomless, much like badly rotten quicksand. If a person were to fall into it, the more they struggled, the quicker they would sink. This sludge of rotting vegetation is at least sixteen feet deep, all of it stinking muck. If dredged, million-year-old bones would be found. Skeletal remains of mammoths and mastodons, extinct animals that once roamed Alaska, a well-known rich history.

On the 25th of July, I fell the tallest white spruce trees peeling them where they fell, to use as pilings for the start of the bridge. I then hauled the logs away from the tree stumps with my ATV, one by one on my new trail. I used the log bob part of my versatile trailer with its two implement sixteen-inch six ply tires, to haul the logs to the bridge location I had previously chosen for a twenty-foot span of water exiting from the lake.

The near side of the outlet's shoreline was relatively grass free but covered by a one-foot thick covering of moss and on the relatively dry firm ground. This nearside shoreline had permafrost beneath the moss and where I was going to start the construction of the bridge. The other side of this twenty-foot span of open water comprised of five-foot tall bear grass growing in the shallow water with permafrost a foot beneath the water. In total, the length of the bridge would be eighty feet, from solid ground to solid ground or shore to shore.

I wanted the decking to be wide enough to support an ATV, so I decided six feet for the bridge's width. I was building it above the tall grass for airflow, which would keep that area under the bridge from collecting heat. If that were to happen, the heat would transfer to the pilings, on down into the permafrost, thus causing the bridge to sink as the permafrost melted.

At the bridge site, the first thing I had to do was find out how far down it was to the top of the permafrost. I did this by driving a probe down at the water's edge, just inside the grass shoreline. The dead spruce pole I used went down easily to the permafrost. The top of the permafrost was deep at the water's edge. I measured it to be twelve feet down. The depth here was due to the heat sink transfer of the grasses and rotting vegetation. Only a few feet inland, the permafrost was only three feet below the surface. The ground cover of thick, dense moss had kept the permafrost closer to the surface here.

Cold water alone does not transfer the heat more than six inches beneath the lake's bottom. The permafrost in Alaska typical is found to be one thousand feet deep. When you see a moose wading in an Alaskan lake, he is not walking in the mud, but standing on the lake's frozen bottom. If a moose is within twelve feet of the shoreline, he is likely in the deep mud and struggling to get further out in the lake, away from the muddy shore.

I probed until I found the shallowest edge of the permafrost to keep the span short as possible. Otherwise, I would have had to back up inland even more, and I did not want to make the span any wider for the diameter and strength of the longest timber logs I had.

Once I knew how deep it was to the permafrost, I could then measure the lengths needed for the two first pilings for the horizontal log of the pier's top and allowing extra length for leveling.

To dig the piling holes, I used a spade. I had to go past the root system and down into the muck to the permafrost. I then placed in each piling dug holes a wide upright plank extending far above for a backstop to guide the piling in unobstructed by the muddy hole and to attach a rope. So that during the raising, and tilting placement of the pilings, the ends would not become stuck. Then once a pole was started, it then slides down into the hole as I raised them on end unobstructed by the muddy edges of the hole.

I had to remove the bark using a drawknife on the logs I had not already skinned. If the bark remains on the log, it will become rotten quickly. A log drawknife is different than a carpenter's drawknife. A carpenter's drawknife is small and flat, with a straight back handle to pull. A log drawknife is longer, with the handles straight out, and the blade is curved to conform to the rounding surface of a log. The handles on it are straight out to the sides, meaning no skinning of the user's hands should they bump them into the log and the handle positioning made for much easier pulling. This draw-knifing was done on a waist-high horizontal log support, as not to give me a backache

To start and to raise the logs took another temporary platform made of short logs stacked in a crib fashion waist-high on the ground back from the post holes, to first tilt the pilings aligning the two base against the strong, tall, wide planked holes. With the help of a small two to three ratio block-and-tackle, like what you may have seen on sailing ships rigging to raise the heavy sails using ropes and winches to aid the sailing crew. I then attached this same block-and-tackle system to the higher end of the tilted piling and the other block to the top of the tall slab.

With the two anchored blocks secured, it was then only a precarious matter of balancing pulling on the haul rope and carefully ever so carefully raise the pilings one by one up on down into the holes. Once the pilings were in the hole and standing on their own, I put my arms around a piling, wiggling, and shoving them down deeper into the watery muck remaining in the hole. They went down easily, then becoming difficult, finally becoming stuck.

My next move was to drive two twelve-inch bridge spikes into the opposite sides of the pilings at my shoulder height but not all the way in leaving four inches for gripping. These four-inch extended spikes were used to lift and drop the pilings until it became too difficult to raise and drop. That was intent labor work. The pilings had not yet reached the hard permafrost. At this point, I used a three-foot heavy log to hammer, driving the pilings deeper, more exercise for me. When finally I heard the pilings ringing sound, meaning I had reached the solid permafrost.

My method was similar to a commercial pile driver; only I was the machine doing the hard labor.

Each piling wide hole was of larger diameter than the piling; this allowed for the easy removal of the slabs and the positioning the angles of the pilings to tilt inward to each other for the pier's final strength. This angle also keeps them from shifting to one side or the other once they are fastened together later.

Once the first two pilings were in place to be the pier base, I measured the tops and sawed off the excess length. Leveling the log ends was done by using a line level, drawing a pen line for preciseness. Now I could place the eight-foot horizontal logs across them. But first, I flattened the underside of the eight-foot horizontal log at the points to be placed on the pilings. The eight-foot horizontal log would extend wider than the decking to come and accommodate the long logs called stringers to place on the next supporting piers until an eighty-foot bridge was complete.

The bridge spikes were only twelve inches, so I had to reduce the thickness of the wood to set the spikes. I did this by hand, auguring large holes into the horizontal log, but only enough to leave four inches of wood to drive the spike through into the pilings. I used a steel punch to drive the twelve-inch bridge spike, thus securing the horizontal log to the piling. Then I made wooden dowel pegs and pounded those into the augured holes to keep the water out. That completed the first pier, which would be used to support the two twenty-five-foot stingers that would cross high above the water, from this pier to the next pier I would be making.

The pier on the other side of the bridge was made the same way; however, at that end I had to float the pilings. Constructing the floating pilings took more time, as I had to use ropes to pull them to the other side of the waterway instead of on location. Because I had no boat to cross the water, I had to make my way down the creek and back up to the construction site with my tools.

Once I had finished with the two main piers, my next step was to lay the bridge stringers across the span of water. They were each twenty-five feet long. The stringer logs needed to be of large diameter, so as they were yet green and bendable by the horizontal span of their weight. I also had to take into consideration the weight of the completed bridge decking and an ATV, when selecting the correct size of stringers. If the ground around the pilings left uncovered, the exposed transferring of heat would quickly sink my hard work taking into account the weight of the bridge.

The log ramp

Engineering the placement of the two log stringers across the span of water and rotten sludge was fun for me, to say the least. To get the stringers in place, I made a portable ramp. Two smaller light logs constructed the two log ramp fasten together side by side was light enough for me to be lifted by hand up onto the second pier. This ramp was now ready to receive the first stringer. The west end was just a short distance out from the first pier and ready to for the stringer to make contact. This narrow ramp's end that rested on the shore would require the utmost of caution in guiding the twenty-five-foot stringers each time one is in place from the pier to pier.

For this task, I used a large four to five ratio block-and-tackle anchoring the one block to the far dry shore that had a tree, the other to a stringer to pull the stringers up to the top of the first pier, aligning them with the pier on the other side of the outlet.

Now that the stringers were resting on the first pier, it was then at that moment I took the time to reflect on the daunting task of building this bridge. Amazingly this bridge construction project was all being put together as I had dreamed. My work never ended even as I slept because each night in my dreams, I was in a separate world, a world that linked to the here and the now. In that world, my grandparents and uncles would give me advice just as they would if they were alive. The dreams and communications I had had been so real, I had a hard time saying goodbye. When I awoke, I knew every aspect of how to proceed, and the finer details would be resolved along the way.

Starting of log upward

A log down on ramp

One by one, I slowly pulled a stringer forward, until at a balancing point far out over the waterway, it would slowly dip down past the balancing point. Once the log tilted beyond the center of the balance point and was above the log ramp guild, that was then a crucial point for me to guide the large balancing stringers and lowering one end onto the log ramp. The stringers' lower end was now near the center of the span of water. This part was a tricky, slippery balancing act. I could not allow a log to surge suddenly downward and fall off this narrow ramp and into the rotting thick sludge. If this were to happen, it would present a problem. I would have to extract it back up out of the muck and have to redo the process. An accident like that would set me back crucial hours. I was very careful to avoid that setback.

The gods were good to me, and my plan worked. It was like I knew what I was doing; my experience had paid off. The two of them were now in place resting on both piers. This accomplishment was a wonderful sight to see.

Logs on piers and ramp view

Yellow raincoat and log

I then spiked the stringers, fastening them. The open waterway was no longer a problem. It was now easier to continue building and completing the eighty-foot bridge.

From the start of construction on July 25 to the first time I was able to drive across the bridge on August 4 at 4:30 p.m. was only ten days. That's all the time it took for me to fall the timber, saw the planks, and nail them together. Add two more days for the cutting of the trail to the bridge building site, making it twelve days total, all of this was accomplished completely on my own.

During the construction of this bridge, I had set up the tripod with the VHS camcorder. I left it on, recording my voice, all the sounds, and a video of the entire process. The captured photos were from my DVD movies for this book.

During these twelve days, I did other things too while I was in the dugout. It seemed as though every day that I was gone, bears would come by to see what I had that they could chew on or knock over. One evening while I was in the dugout, I glanced up at the door and could see the light shining in. Daylight! A bear had been on the sod roof and had clawed a small hole, removing material in its attempt to gain entrance.

That morning, I took a few hours off from bridge building to building a stockade around the roof, to keep bears from getting on the roof and ripping a hole to come down inside. The thought of coming home from work to find a bear trapped inside would not have ended in an outcome that would have been good for neither the bear nor me.

Pancakes

The first meal of the day, I ate was a stack of five large thick full plate-size pancakes with a covering of butter and a layer of brown sugar on each. These high energy pancakes kept me invigorated all day and perhaps helped me dream. For the suppers, I made up one of Larry's delicious, stomach-filling, super spicy hot dishes in a tall porcelain camper stew pot. These meals lasted me two suppers every two days. Oh, and by the way, please don't tell anyone, but I ate right out of the stew pot. Seldom did I wash dishes; this saved me a lot of time. Every third day, I made a new hot dish, which seemed to become even more flavorful as the days went by, from not washing the stew pot.

Oh, by the way, if you ever run out of pancake syrup, like I did, brown sugar is even better than syrup. I was fortunate to have included the twenty-five-pound bag of brown sugar in the supplies Larry and I brought up; it turned out to be my substance of life, packed with energy.

CHAPTER 11

Black Bear Warning

I must make myself abundantly clear. No one must ever trust a bear. There are no two bears alike in their looks or demeanor. A bear can kill you with one swing of their paw and then eat you. Perhaps because at this time while living alone, my bear encounters did not involve anyone's safety but myself. Had I had anyone living with me, I would not have tolerated interactions of a bear. Therefore, I will discuss my inappropriate interactions with a bear in an upcoming chapter. In no way do I condone my actions with a single bear, let alone more than one. I am simply sharing my history and expressing not to repeat my same mistake. A bear can be the gentlest animal on earth one second, and in an instant, they can transform into a deadly powerful beast. A bear does not read, nor know human laws. The only laws they understand is survival. But like a human, a bear can become a belligerent freeloader expecting handouts. Bears will take what they want whenever they want, boldly or as a thief in the night.

Alaska has an average of four human deaths a year by black bears.

Newly born moose are the easiest of prey for a black bear. A pregnant moose, once sighted by a bear or wolf, is followed and hounded until the newborn has appeared. The bears and wolves keep the moose population from exploding as is nature's way. Predator and prey create a balance in the circle of life. Many moose hunters feel cheated by this natural balance. It can have a direct effect on the number of hunting licenses the state issues for both residents and nonresidents. A lower moose count population affects the tourism industry as well. However, hunting guilds do have spring bear hunts that make up for some of the loss in business from the wild competition.

I have had enough good and bad interactions with the bear to have come to understand their nature, and that it's possible to live with them, but keeping a safe distance. Never feed a bear, befriend them, or leave anything available that can be damaged by a bear. Some of the things bears are drawn to include anything petroleum-based, such as tires, rubber, cushions, plastics, oil, greases, and or even drying clothes hung a line outdoors.

I have learned while living in the remote wilderness the easiest way to live in harmony with a bear is to keep anything that I do not want eaten, or chewed, squirrely stored. That is but one reason I was including a drive in the secured basement in the house plans. Most homeowners in this region build bear-proof outbuildings for storage. Bear-proof doors and windows must be installed anywhere that is within reachable distance of a bear. The coverings should be made to cover totally the windows and doors, allowing no space to see through the inside. The coverings should be made to be quickly added or removed in the case of having to leave on short notice.

Bear board spike portable mats made by driving long sharp nails through the underside of a board spaced in one-and-a-half-inch increments. These bear boards are laid on the steps, below windows or in front of an entry door in place of a welcome mat. Then if a bear tries to get into the building, and they step on the sharp nail mat, the mat will cause the bear bandit to back away.

If a bear finds even the slightest give in a covered window or boarded door, they will use their weight to pounce on the weak spot, until their momentum and weight cause the blockade to fail. Once the bear can get inside, they will trash everything in the dwelling, finding a different way to exit, by the same means as their entrance. In all my experience, a bear never once has exited the same way they entered.

Had I not learned how to live with the local bear, instead of killing them, I would have been consumed with the task of processing the meat, or disposing of it. I could have easily had killed up to eleven bears in a single summer. Now that would become overwhelming.

CHAPTER 12

Mr. Bear, Boo-Boo, Fuzzy, and Wink

The following bear interactions occurred during a time when I was alone. When I did have visitors of the human kind, the bears seemed to know to keep out of sight. All these encounters with the four bears ended in no harm to me. About every day I was visited by a bear, but never more than one at a time. The bears were taking their turns in visiting me.

During my time building the eighty-foot bridge, some bears were always checking out my dugout. I knew better than to leave things out for them to chew. I would even leave the radio on to trick them into thinking I was home, but it made no difference. Before long, the bears became accustomed to the voices on the radio and lost any fear that would have kept them at bay. In the end, the radio became nothing more than entertainment for them.

Mr. Bear

Bear biting window

Wednesday, August 5, the day after the bridge competition, I intended to sleep in late. Instead, at 7:30 a.m., I was abruptly awakened by a loud thump on the window. The window is of triple pane Plexiglas. If the window was made of real glass, it would have been smashed in by the bears not long after I installed it.

I jumped off the bunk and dashed to the door. Through the window, I could see the black bear running away toward the outhouse.

I was dressed only in my shorts when I opened the door and stepped outside. I called out in a mellow tone of voice, just as he was about to pass the outhouse. "Hello, bear, what's the matter? Come on back. I will not hurt you." In one hand I held the camcorder, my other was holding my grandfather's .32 Remington pump brush rifle. I had turned the camcorder on a while back in the dugout and managed to catch this bear event on film.

I brought along the rifle and the camcorder mainly for preparation should I encounter any of the Little People. I wanted to capture one or more of these elusive beings on film. I had vowed that I would never kill one after I had come to understand them. I had seen this being a few times in earlier days, and the rifle was for backup, but in time, I lost my fear of the Hairy Ones.

Bear walking

The bear stopped, turned carefully around, and looked up at me. Again, I said in an easy calming tone of voice, "Come, I wouldn't hurt you. What are you up to, bear? It's a bit early for me, are you hungry? I will be fixing breakfast soon."

The bear casually walked back toward me. The bear was now between the outhouse and me, looking about as he walked from side to side, and then looking back at me. His ears were up normal, and his hair was flat. He was showing no signs of aggression. If his ears were laid back, and his hackles raised, I would have understood his warning of ill intent from his defensive posture.

I kept talking in a friendly voice and made no sudden moves. I watched every movement of his ever so slow and deliberate steps, as he approached me. To me not to have a rifle in my hands or a gun on my hip is to be naked clothes on or not. But in this case, I was wearing only shorts and holding a rifle.

I set the rifle down, leaving it near the dugout's closed door, and kept it right close to me, to grasp fast if needed. Both safeties were off, and the rifle was ready to fire.

Grandfather's rifle was antique, which had two on-off safety switches. One of those safeties was an off-on slide switch on the breach action, and the other was a trigger safety, which had a two-way push button.

Bear looking at me

I looked at the bear; we were going to have a few words. "We're on the same side of the door now, aren't we?" That was no small bear. He was a full-grown adult; he could have weighed up to four hundred pounds. This bear makes no sound, but he was eyeing the dugout over, especially the door. I knew what he was thinking. I could read his mind. He wanted to know how to get into this newly discovered "den."

His large padded feet made no sounds as he moved around. The soft leather padding on his feet was similar to a person wearing moccasins, allowing for quiet stealth.

Bears nose on the edge of door

The bear brought his nose to the bottom of the door and sniffed, inhaling loudly. He was sniffing the scents from within the dugout. He was exploring what he could with his nose while eyeing the edges of the door. I was standing near the edge of the door, blocking the bear's way. Without any hesitation, the bear simply pressed his cold nose against my leg and gently nudged me off to the side.

The eight feet high door let me know how long he was. He stood on his hind feet, placed his forepaws on top of the door, and looked up at the roof line in a curious way, by stretching his neck. Looking at the bear I had an aha moment; I realized that he was the culprit that had tried to dig his way in through the roof—convinced my conclusion was accurate when I noticed the bear was looking right at the patched hole.

Bear standing up at the door

While he was standing on his hind feet with his paws on top the door, I realized he was three feet taller than me. The bear turned and looked down at me. Mind you, in my bare feet, I stand at 6'1". Four hundred pounds of a living bear standing alongside me was a wee bit intimidating.

He backed up enough to lower his forepaws to the bottom of the door's windows frame, where the massive center hinge was on the door he used his claws to grip the long wooden hinge and pulled the door open. The bear was excited at his discovery; he began to open and close the door at will. He glanced at me as if to say, "This is fun!"

Keep in mind, all this time, I was inches away next to him. I remained by the opening of the door, to make a hasty retreat inside if need be and, of course, bringing along the rifle.

The bear studied the door's operation like a kid would with a new toy. He was getting the hang of swinging the door open and closed, a look of glee in his beady black eyes.

He soon grew bored with just swinging the door back and forth and proceeded to push the door wide open, with a strong thrust. He proceeded to push now the door wide open from the inside face of the door with a strong thrust. I had made the door similar to a bank door, sturdy and heavy, but with a window.

I had to tell him sternly, "*No! No, bear, no!*" He was testing the limits of the wood hinges, pushing the door as far as he could. The door stood wide open, pushed outward and against the outside of the dugout. There was nothing stopping him from going inside.

"That is enough, bear. Step back so I can close the door." I used a commanding voice so he would know I was serious. The bear stepped back and seemed to understand my displeasure. A stern tone of voice works as a universal language; tone of voice is understood, even if the language is not.

When I closed the door, the bear watched how I operated it and wanted to do that too. The fancy natural gnarled tree root used for pulling the door caught his eye that right away. This bear's mind was now really working. The only thing I did not demonstrate was how to work the locking latch mechanism. I had no desire for him to learn that trick too.

This bear was a top-notched student; his eyes were followed on my every move, taking in all the details. If I were to grade his test scores, I am sure I would have marked them with straight As.

Whenever I was home in the dugout, and my daily chores had me going in and out, I would leave the door unlatched for convenience.

This bear was smart; I think I could have employed him on a work-for-food basis.

"Well, Mr. Bear, that's the name I will call you. Mr. Bear, I have to fix breakfast and get dressed. It's cold out here." I went inside and only pulled the door closed, but left it unlatched. I looked out through the window and watched him sniffing around my empty tin cans, licking them shiny clean. Yes, I had a messy yard. I would clean that up, right after I ate my pancakes.

Necessity is the mother of invention, and this bit of wisdom had been proven true for me in the past. There was a time I ran out of syrup for my pancakes, and being 145 air miles from the nearest store, I had to make do with the supplies I had on hand. I tried brown sugar and discovered I loved it. Maybe it was the tasty brown sugar, but my love of pancakes covered in butter, and layered with a heavy amount of brown sugar, wasn't satisfied until I had finished five pancakes for each of those meals.

Mr. Bear was still hanging around. It was not that he was starving. I knew beyond a doubt that Mr. Bear was perfectly capable of fending for himself, being the wild animal he was. But he looked so disappointed that my cans were mostly clean of any food. While I watched him scrounging for leftovers, I had a flashback of my time in Korea seeing orphans some of which maimed from the war and later from the live remaining explosives. These children seemingly on their own were trying to live by scrambling about for any scraps that they could get from us soldiers while we were passing by in a convoy handing out to them whatever we had. Suddenly as in Korea, it dawned on me that I had some food under my table, I have a big stockpile of canned beans among the other canned foods. I had much more than I would ever eat this year. I selected a can of Van Camp's pork and beans and opened it up.

I pushed the door open and set the rifle down within easy reach. I went back in and grabbed my bulky camcorder, turning it on. I held it in one hand, beans in the other, as I went out to continue my conversation with Mr. Bear. "Come here. I have something that I know you will like." Boy! I didn't have to tell him twice! His eyes fixed on that can of cold beans, with his big nose sniffing and twitching from right to left.

Bear eating beans

Not far off to the side of my small front yard, I had a homemade wooden animal cage, which Jeff Peterson had made the year before. We had used it to hold a wounded marten while it healed, that I had shot by a .22cal rifle bullet, and we nursed it back to health and kept it as a pet. Now the box would be used as a dining table for Mr. Bear.

"Hold on, bear, wait and mind your manners." Bear was sticking his nose in the can before I could pour the beans on the top of the table.

After I had poured the beans around in a wide arc, I left the empty can on the table, thinking he would like to lick it clean after the main course.

I watched him eat and filming the ways of a bear made me familiar with the many of their habits. A bear never stands to eat, when he can sit to eat. Mr. Bear liked to eat popcorn, but his preferred dining habit was to lie on the ground and suck up the popcorn like a vacuum cleaner. He would stick out his tongue like an anteater and inhale the popcorn treat.

That was the first time I had fed a bear a can of beans. He started out standing on all fours, eventually sitting on the ground with his head laid on the table. Bear was just shoveling it in with his slurping tongue. I mean to tell you, this bear had no table manners. He was making continued slobbering slurping sounds like there was no tomorrow.

His tabletop soon was licked clean. There was no need to wash the tabletop after he had licked it. Next, he went on to lick the empty bean can. The bean can slid off the table. Bear was determined to clean the can. To keep the can from moving away from him, he put one impressive paw on it to hold it in place.

Mr. Bear gave the can several thorough inspections before determining there was nothing more to taste. That's when he turned his attention back to me. "*Bear…that was…sixty-four ounces of beans. You can't be hungry anymore.*" He was.

At this point, I used hand signs and told him, "No more, all gone!" I did this by placing the palms of my hands together and rubbing them, and then shook them apart. Mr. Bear understood that.

Bear had come to learn my tone of voice whether I was displeased, mellow, or otherwise safe to be around. And I'll be darned if he didn't quickly understand sign language.

I decided to go back inside the dugout because it appeared bear was going to be leaving. He headed off for a bit, but it wasn't long before he showed back up again. He was starting to become a pest, a potential problem. I would have to get him to understand when his welcome was worn out, and when it was time for him to leave. How could I do that without harming him or endangering myself? The answer to this dilemma was slowly developing in my mind.

The next time Mr. Bear came back, I thought, *That's it. I have to deal with this now.* It was time to bring out the big rifle. Not to kill Mr. Bear but to fire it and scare him away with the load noise.

The big rifle was the 8mm Mauser, a German rifle. The .32 Remington rifle is big too, but they had stopped making the casings and the bullets for that gun, so I didn't want to use the hard-to-replace ammo when I had the 8mm Mauser with readily available bullets.

Outside the dugout, I was armed with the 8mm rifle. I scolded Bear, telling him to go. He didn't move. He just stood there wanting food. With both my hands on the long rifle, I thrust it broadside raising it at him and said, "Go! I have no more, go!"

At a distance of twenty feet, I took careful aim and fired over his head. *Boom!* Bear had absolutely no reaction to the loud boom. It was at this point I realized this bear had never before experienced a hunter with a rifle, and for sure had no idea of what a rifle could do. Man! This bear needs an education. Mr. Bear will not live two minutes if a bear hunter sees him. I wanted him to see a bullet plow into the ground. I fire again, this time by his feet. I was reminded now of the western movies on how they will have a cowboy do the "bullet dance."

Even the bullet has plowed up dirt onto the bear's face; it did not deter him. "Houston, I have a problem." I knew this was a problem I would have to deal with on my own.

I have been hunting bears for years in Canada, none posed for me to kill them. I scratched my head to force an idea from my small brain; it worked like a light bulb snapped on a brilliant idea came to me. Well, then this next idea should work. I walked up to Mr. Bear, placed the muzzle of the rifle alongside one of his ears six inches away to shoot past him. The report of the bullet leaving the muzzle the concussion will temperately hurt his ear, and he would run away.

That should do the trick. *Boom!*

Not even as much as a blink or flinch did he make!

Okay, I give up. This bear did not have a clue what a gun was nor was he picking up on my obvious clues. He did not appear to be angry or even bewildered; he was calm and cool. Mr. Bear had learned to trust me; his only interest was in finding a snack.

By now I had given up, calling it a bad cause. Bear would leave on his own given time. I had things to do. I went inside to finish preparing for a day of work ahead.

Once I was safely inside, I looked out to see Mr. Bear was making a fuss. Picking up the camcorder, I took a motion picture of this temper tantrum through the safety of the window. Mr. Bear, the king of the forest, turned and approached the window looking at me watching him. He displayed his hunger pains in a way that I learned something I had never known before or would have ever thought. A bear can spread his jaws fully open and bite the flat plastic glass window. His huge sharp teeth gouged his signature in my Plexiglas window.

Bear opening door

I heard a creaking of the door, then felt a draft. I turned just in time to see the door creeping opening. I had the lens focused on the opening of the door and filmed as a wide paw with extended claws was pulling the door open. Bear with one widespread open paw with extended claws was pulling the door open. I moved to the door and yanked it back closed, saying "*No!*" I quickly latched it, locking the door.

Bear was not planning on leaving me alone anytime soon; that much was clear. So much for getting any work done, I had a big-time bear problem to take care of instead of work.

My first mistake was inviting the bear, but my biggest mistake was in feeding the bear.

There are many people that consider killing a bear, no big deal. Just shoot the bear and, using an ATV, drag him off far away, or skin and butcher it on site. None of these were realistic options for me. First of all, I had named him. Second, he had come to trust me to do him no harm. Third, I had no way to preserve the meat. Fourth, I had no spare time to deal with a dead bear. Oh sure, I could gut shoot him and see him run off to die two hills away, easy and done with, right?

But that was not me; I do not treat any living being that way. If I had been a young man immature in my youth, I might have had the idea to kill the bear. I have no problem killing for food or self-defense, but killing without reason was not something I was going to do.

Mr. Bear was clawing the door, trying to pull it open. Reluctantly, I opened the door a little bit, just enough for me to extend out a hand. I held out a hunk of block cheese to Mr. Bear. He liked the cheese. Bear was gently eating it while I held the cheese in my hand.

Bear eating cheese from my hand

The camcorder was still rolling. Carefully, he had eaten it all and finished by licking my fingers clean one by one. I could feel his taste buds, but not once did I feel his teeth, nor did he break my skin. I was surprised at how gentle he was, even though my hand had been far enough in his mouth to touch his tonsils. He backed off and acted like he had manners, like he was saying thank you for asking me for more. *Oh no*, I thought, *now what?* I closed the door to give me a chance to think.

My brain kicked into gear, and I came up with an idea I was sure had to work. Just to the inside of the doors opening, I had shelves stocked with spices for cooking. I opened the door and peeked out. Bear was looking at me through the gap in the door. He looked happy to see me.

"Bear, you're still hungry I see. Let me see what I have?" I was kneeling down while talking to Mr. Bear through the door's small opening. I grabbed my blue metal camper's cup off one of the shelves.

I looked the shelf over, a bottle of Tabasco sauce was standing out in full view. I grabbed it and said, "Ah-ha, thanks," to my guardian angel. I poured an inch of tobacco in the cup and held it out for Mr. Bear. Bear quickly without hesitation extended his eight-inch tongue, curling it down into the bottom of the cup. All in one motion, his tongue soaked up the sauce like it was a sponge. Bear left his tongue lolling out.

I watched his delayed reaction during the time it took for the hot sauce to go with his tongue to his brain; it was like watching a flickering flame turning into a full-grown blaze. His tongue remained fully extended, but his itty-little-bitty beady black eyes flew opened wide, his extra-large eyes revealed a look of horror at the extreme pain.

Bear was in excruciating pain, but even that didn't hide his bewilderment. Bear immediately stepped back, with his tongue fully extended out, wagging it. He began to shake his tongue wildly, never once retracting it back in his mouth while making a loud, continuous *oooh, oooh* sound with every breath he took. He turned and trotted off making his mournful *oooh, oooh* cries as he disappeared off into the distance. I can only assume he was running down to the cold spring in the valley.

It was eight days before Bear came back. In his absence, he had learned to use caution and would sniff, taste to eat with manners. When he finished eating what I would provide for him, he would leave without argument, and thus we became friends. I kept a full bowl of popped popcorn on hand, ready to pass out to him and the other bears.

Living by oneself does not always mean that person is alone. Living in the remote wilderness gives the opportunity for many animal friends. Most animals were shy, but none was afraid of me. I found that to earn the respect of the animals, I had first to show them respect.

The shyest of all the animals I encountered were the ones Alaskan Natives refer to as the the Little People, the creatures I spoke of earlier in this book, the creatures I know as the Hairy Ones. But even these evasive and bashful beings respected me, as I respected them. The Hairy Ones had a way of letting me know they had been in my yard; they would place a heavy length of firewood across the pathway to the outhouse, where they seemed to know I would be walking daily. A chunk of firewood placed in the same, approximate place. Not anywhere else. They were consistent in doing this. The woodpile was thirty feet from the path, and I would commonly find a hefty size length of firewood placed intentionally in the center of the trail. It became their trademark or calling card.

Whenever the Hannans came to visit, they always had a dog or two they brought along. A bear had never shown during all their visits. Dennis saw my recordings of the bear and told me. "Someday, Duane, I might find your camcorder has recorded a bear eating you." Dennis was not kidding.

Bears pose a very real, deadly threat and can approach out of nowhere at any time. That is the reason I always carried a gun. I did not rely on pepper spray, air horns, bells, or a big stick. All those kinds of defenses are unreliable and give the holder a false sense of confidence, which could cause them to drop their guard, making them even more vulnerable. Mind you, most bears do not know what a gun is, or what the sound *bang* represents. A gun should be used only to kill, not to wound or cause suffering, and because of this, a gun should only be used as a last resort.

Boo-Boo

Boo-Boo's name comes from his physical description and funny mannerisms. This bear did not look like a typical black bear, in that he was shorter in length, with a rounder body but most notably short, stunted legs. I would guess his age to be over two years.

Boo-Boo liked his treats too, but other than being somewhat shy, he was well mannered, and I had no problems with him.

Big bears are too heavy to climb trees. The younger ones have no problem in scampering up a tree. Boo-Boo looked and behaved like a clown. He found enjoyment in scaring the crap out of me. When he succeeded in scaring m, he would make a laughing sound, swaying his head and his body from side to side.

Boo-Boo's only unwelcome habit was to surprise me when I was walking on a trail by dropping out of a tree and landing in front of me. He would do it to me anywhere, anytime, but always when I was least expecting it. Whenever he would surprise me this way, it felt like my heart stopped. The first time he dropped in front of me, my response was "Geeze, Boo-Boo, you scared the heck out of me." He shook himself off and walked away, making his *hoo-hoo* laughing sound. He headed nonchalantly down the trail ahead of me, without looking back.

Once I realized Boo-Boo's trick wasn't a one-time affair, my tone changed, and I would shout at him, "*Stop doing that!*"

Fuzzy

Fuzzy was another bear visitor on Ose Mountain. As you may have guessed, his nickname came from the way his hair grew bent on the ends. When I first pondered a name for him, I briefly thought of Curly, but his hair was like a magnet collecting burrs and bark, just like Velcro.

Fuzzy was well mannered and young. Young bears tend to be more inclined to be vandals making trouble, getting into everything and causing destruction. Fuzzy was an exception; the king of the forest, Mr. Bear, must have warned the other bears to be on their best behavior when they visited me, lest they get their tongue burned by a hot treat.

Wink

Another small bear that visited me, I named Wink. Wink was well behaved, but by no means shy. He would continuously blink his eyes, hence the name. Every time he would show up for a treat, his eyes would flutter open and close, over and over, as if to dislodge something. I looked his eyes over for some irritant or an eyelash stuck in his eye, but his eyes were clear and bright. I did notice. However, he was hard of sight. He had to be closer than the other bears when he ate his treats, to see them. His nose leads him more than his eyes.

Wink needed eyeglasses. It became evident to me in the days following his first visit, when there was no end to his blinking and squinting. One day when Wink was visiting, blinking away, I thought of the girls at the reception desk at my eye doctor's office. I imagined the looks on their faces, as I walked in with Wink by my side. "Hi, girls, my friend here needs an eye exam." Perhaps an operation to correct the vision is in order? That might be the only way for him to see well. Ho, it is okay, he trusts me, and well behaves. Just do not pet him, for some reason, he doesn't like to be touched that way. Give him a treat, and you'll win his heart over."

I would have paid real money to have made that dream a reality, but there would have been a problem in convincing my pilot. Even if he agreed, Wink might not have felt comfortable in being secured in a safety harness in the back seat of the plane. Wink would have preferred to be in the front. Nope, if I had lived by a road maybe, but to fly him into town was out of the question. *Rats!*

CHAPTER 13

The Hannan Homesteaders

Dennis and Jill each have their own federal homestead that is spaced about one mile apart, but live in one. Dennis had completed his homestead first. Dennis's homestead is inland in the boreal tundra forest back a good mile from the lake they used.

Even though Dennis had completed his homestead first, I write about Jill's homestead first. Because when I was brought over by canoe there for the first time, Jill wanted me to see her unfinished place before the end of the day as we would be back to Dennis's, where they presently lived. Jill wanted to be sure I saw everything that day, knowing I might not be back for whatever reason. After all, travel time in the wilderness took a vast amount of time.

Jill's homestead had one of her four property lines a hundred feet back from the high-water mark of the tundra pond she settled near. A setback of a hundred feet of the high-water mark was a requirement of the federal government. Four feet had made each of Jill's property lines wide cleared lanes, which she and Dennis had accomplished. Jill's homestead property measured 660 feet by 360 feet, five acres total.

Jill had chosen to stake her property on the shoreline of a typical shallow Alaskan tundra pond they call a lake. A lake allows them nine to ten months of the year's accessibility by an airplane. The months of ice forming or melting limits the use of a lake. For those months, the lake is not safe to land a plane; the Hannans are totally isolated and must prepare for emergencies and food.

The Hannans decided to call the lake Dead Fish Lake, after they found the remains of a mudminnow. These fish are called bonefish by the Alaskan natives; the fish are small but have a lot of bones. Mudminnows range in size, with the larger ones getting up to eight inches in length. They have one long dorsal fin, which extends back to the tail and up their belly, making it strange in appearance. The natives used to trap these fish long ago, using a type of wood weaved funnel trap. They used the fish to feed their dogs. Mudminnows are also a favorite of land otters, who thrive on the fish that live in the tundra ponds. They swim in schools and survive the long cold winters by burrowing into the lake's muddy bottom, although some fish don't survive and is most likely what caused the fate of the fish the Hannans discovered. That can happen during winters where the ice is extremely thick.

Most types of fish would never survive if they remained in a shallow pond in the winter months, due to the lack of oxygen. Although I have known northern pike to survive in these waters in a similar manner, they can slow down their heart rate and thereby need less oxygen. Most pike migrate to deeper water before the season changes to winter, sealing the lake with ice and limiting the oxygen.

These tundra ponds were formed by the melting of the glacial ice fields ten thousand years ago, and perhaps many times before. Earth's forever changing weather maintains the cycle of life; thus far the weather is the one uniqueness our planet has. People seldom look to the sun for our earth's weather and take the sun for granted. Our sun is an uncontrollable ball of fire, which can heat up or cool at will. In time, the sun will come overheated, burning out, as all the stars do, but by the time that happens, the earth will have been burned to a cinder, void of water and life.

The Hannans had two young sons, Shaun and Stormy. We were able to visit each other's homesteads by a few different means of traveling. We could walk by following both wet and dry trails, or we could take a canoe to a creek and across a lake dividing us. We had jointly decided to call this lake Long Lake. I still remember the vision of Jill carrying a very young Stormy in a backpack carrier traveling to visit.

We communicated daily with the Hannans using the citizens band radio on the AM channel 5. The CB was our only means of communicating. We each had an AM/FM radio to keep us informed as to what is happening in the world, but mostly the AM/FM radio was used for tuning into Trapline Chatter KGNP, of North Pole, Alaska, for any incoming messages.

How Dennis and Jill became a couple is a story to write, but they did share much of their captivating history with me. Dennis had served in the navy and, therefore, qualified for all the benefits a veteran was due under the Federal Homestead Act of 1862. That included having to put in less time on his property to be approved, than a nonveteran citizen. Jill, on the other hand, had to put in the full amount of time required to meet the federal guidelines, termed "proving up," to get her habitable dwelling approved. I am proud to tell you she accomplished that goal.

Dennis and Jill did their homework preparing for their move to the wilderness. They lived in their pickup truck, which had a topper, working odd jobs and managing a motel in Fairbanks. They saved their money for materials flown to their claims. What is even more outstanding is that they managed to prove up their homestead while having to fly back and forth from the lake to town, working in both places, giving birth to two healthy sons.

Stormy, the youngest, was born earlier than his expected due date. They had no name picked or agreed upon before birth. The hospital requires parents to have a name on a newborn's birth certificate before they can be released. Jill and Dennis looked at each other, and out the window at the stormy weather, and hence his name came to be Stormy.

The Hannans lived off the land, hunting and fishing, along with gardening foods they could grow. Dennis supplemented his income by being a proficient trapper and an excellent fur handler. A local fur buyer, whom I shall leave unnamed, would fly out with supplies, charging for the trip as well and buy up Dennis's furs. Dennis was not well compensated, barely breaking even for his expert abilities in trapping and his fur handling of valuable furs in my opinion, but perhaps that is not for me to say.

Jill and Dennis tanned hides and made things from them, along with other crafts to sell in the tourist shops.

Jill was incredibly talented in her ways too. She excelled at making all types and sizes of birch baskets; Jill knew which birch trees would work best, as well as the ideal time for harvesting the bark. She would use roots from spruce trees splitting the roots into strings to use for stitching in her baskets. Jill was always very forthcoming and willing to share the tricks of her trade.

It was quite some time after we became neighbors and friends before I first saw the Hannans' home. I will never forget it. I awoke at 9:30 a.m. and skipped breakfast. A morning rain was coming down, but it had begun before 7:00 a.m. so it would quite before eleven, and it did. A proven farming saying I had learned in my youth. "Rain before seven will be quite before eleven."

I had some chores to do that morning before I planned to head out and meet with Jill and Dennis at Long Lake. Like closing in with planks, my full Rubbermaid water-filled barrels, this was exposed and unprotected from the bears. I stored my ATV in the smokehouse for the same reason; I didn't wish to come home and discover it made into a chew toy. I took a cold shower in the shower house Larry and I had built.

The blue shower house

I decide to fancy myself up a bit and wear the clothes I had for my time traveling on the Alaska-Canadian Highway. I put on my western hat and buckskin leather long fringed jacket. My long leather jacket was a homemade gift from my brother Mike, who was into buck skinning at that time. It was a beautiful piece of work, tanned from the raw hide of a white-tailed deer. Mike was a Civil War actor, a musket shooter, and a collector of antiques of that period.

I could now begin my walk down the hill and around Levi Lake to meet the couple on the southwestern inward corner shore of Long Lake.

Dennis and Jill waited at my end of what was newly established and was called the trail head of the Long Lake's shoreline. They patiently waited for two and a half hours while I journeyed to find them. The area at the trail head is thick with solid trees right up to the water's edge. It turns out I had missed the trailhead and was temporarily confused about my location. It wasn't that I became lost in the thick woods; I just took a bit of a detour, as this was an area of wilderness I was unfamiliar with at that time. I remind you this area is of solid trees right to the water's edge.

I eventually made my way to the lake by following the sound of ducks and seagulls. As I was emerging from the thick growth at the shore, I faintly heard someone calling my name in the distance. I looked all around, spotting them on the faraway shoreline I had passed. I responded calling out to them, before heading in their direction. I had to trudge my way through a tangled mess of virgin forest swampland next to the shore to keep from becoming confused again.

Needless to say, an ATV trail is cut and cleared leading to this trailhead in the days to follow by all of us.

I apologized for being late, and they stated they quite well understood. They were familiar with the North American jungle I had to go through to find them.

For the place to beach the canoe, Dennis had found an old clear and precise narrow now dry waterway. That at one time had emptied water into the lake. That once waterway perhaps was formed a million years ago by melting glaciers and was now used only during an unusually heavy rain. That was a perfect landing and trailhead site. This trailhead made for easy accessibility and was only a short distance to deep water to float a canoe readily. The rest of the high banked shoreline to either side was comprised of tall grasses and littered with fallen trees both in the watery grasses and on land. This lake was not a typical resort beach.

Lake View with Denali backdrop

Jill climbed in the canoe first and went forward to the bow. I handed her my pack, Grandfather's rifle, and the camcorder, then I climbed in and sat in the canoe's center. Dennis asked us, "Are you ready?"

Dennis was wearing waders, so he pushed us away from the shore. Once the canoe was afloat, Dennis climbed in, and we were off. Jill and Dennis were excellent canoe paddlers. Methodically rowing in sync, their paddles sliced through the water. There was only the sound of water drops falling from the ends of the paddles as they're raised out of the water before they were once again silently sliced below the surface, propelling us forward. We glided smoothly across the water, enjoying each other's company. That was my first time out on Long Lake, so I peered over the edge of the canoe to see what was beneath the water's surface. "This lake is not very deep, is it?"

Jill replied, "No, it's not. If it weren't for the weeds growing up, you could see the bottom. It makes for good food for the moose, though."

Dennis turned to me with a wink in his eye. "Those weeds are a place for the northern pike to hide and hunt."

"You got that right." Thinking about the northern pike brought to mind an experience I had back once another nearby lake. "Back at Levi Lake, I once seen a full-grown duck get swallowed by a gator-sized pike. One moment I was watching a duck swimming, the next there was a big swirl in the water, and I saw big teeth lining with open jaws, and the duck was gone. I stopped dangling my toes in the lake after that."

We were passing close to the first point of land jutting into the lake on our right, when I said, "You know, this would be a good place for me to stand up and pan the camcorder around for effect."

Jill quickly retorted, "*No, Duane*, not a good idea."

Dennis said, "Only if you want to get wet, Duane."

"I know, I know. I just had to hear what you'd say about the film as I am recording all this." I laughed.

By this time, we were passing the second point of land jutting out, this one on our left, and preceded on to the drainage outlet of the lake, where a twenty-foot wide creek began. We traveled short ways into the creek and came upon an active beaver lodge; they had built a tall home, which had cozy-muck plants growing all over it.

"Look, Jill. That's a healthy stand of cozy-muck for you to harvest."

"What is that, Duane?"

"Cozy-muck, it's wild rhubarb. In the early days of mankind, the native Alaskans collected the red stalks, pulling the stalks popping them from the base of the plant, and cutting the leafy top ends off. But saving the leaf tops to cover individual, family-sized mound serving piles that a family would eat in a short time. Sort of like canning, one pile is used at a time. Making many piles covered first by its leaves and later by a lot of snow insulating the stalks from freezing. They utilized nature and had the luxury of fresh greens to eat longer in the latter season of winter.

We pulled up alongside the old beaver house of growing cozy-muck and picked some to eat. "Yes, that's sweet, and good, thanks, Duane."

"The redder the stalk is, the better the taste is, Jill."

We were startled by a loud screeching noise; the canoe bottom scraped right over a beaver wood cache as we traveled along. "Boy, we just scraped over that!" I remarked. A beaver cache for food is made of fresh green hardwood saplings, forced at their ends into the muddy bottom to stay there. Stacking and storing the wood beneath the surface meant fresh wood and easy under the surface access during the cold winter. A beaver can hold their breath long enough to eat underwater for long periods of time or bite off a section to eat inside the house.

Like beaver, moose eat wood too, so if I want to harvest a moose anytime during the winter with easy distance from the house, I stack a pile of green treetops with the leaves on earlier in the fall, and all winter the moose will feed on the pile until it's all gone. I call moose feeding in the yard walking meat markets. Dennis remarked, "Good idea, Duane."

We continued our short journey, the canoe taking us along the creek's meandering, twisting, and turning path, surrounded by tall marsh grasses growing along both banks. As we floated around a bend in the creek, I could hear the splashing resonance of running water nearby. As the weeds cleared ahead, we spotted the source of the sounds. There was a beaver dam ahead, and it had created a spillway, giving us a privet symphony of waterfall melodies. Without hesitation, Dennis and Jill paddled the canoe forward, straight toward the spillway. Dennis quietly told me, "Hang on, Duane." The canoe plunged forward until its tipping point, and the canoe suddenly tipped downward, when *swoosh*, we were below the spillway of the beaver dam.

"That was *fun!* We have to do that again sometime."

Dennis then said, "Well, Duane, you will when you go home, but coming back, we will have to get out and portage the canoe up over it."

The creek with grasses on its sides

As we continued, the creek narrowed until it became just a trickle, and we stopped. Dennis jumped out, since he had waders on, and pulled the canoe while Jill and I pushed with the paddles. When we reached solid ground, we were able to exit the canoe without getting wet. Dennis hid the canoe in the woods far back from the creek's edge, out of sight.

From here we walked on a narrow muskeg trail, with black scraggly spruce trees growing on either side. The pathway was dark surrounded by entangled and grown-over foliage. The ground covered with moss was growing on the frozen permafrost ground. This trail had been heavily used by the Hannans and had sunken in.

Dennis took point

Dennis took the point, I was next, and Jill walked behind me.

That was inland silvertip grizzly country, their favored hunting grounds, so we were alert as we proceeded. We seemed to be walking for quite some distance, when I turned to Dennis and like a kid on a car trip asked, "How much further?"

And much like a parent responding to the child, Dennis said, "We're almost there now, Duane."

About then, we heard dogs barking in the distance. They'd heard Dennis and me talking. Jill spoke up, "Yup, that's Chena. She heard us and got the others going."

Hannans' house

The Perimeter

The trail entered a wide open span of cleared ground, which Dennis called the Compound. There were a few selected trees growing around the open area, trees that had been missed by a wildfire in the years past. The fire-killed trees had been moved back, forming a kind of fence, a barrier so to speak. Dennis referred to the piles of dead trees as the Perimeter!

Dennis and Jill had built their habitable dwelling of plywood painted white. All the material had been flown in and offloaded from a small float plane. They used Dead Fish Lake for the plane to land on, located about a half mile from their homestead.

The dwelling was small in size, similar to a Minnesota ice fishing house. That kept the extremely cold air limited to the arctic entrance room. After the door to the entrance was closed, the final door was next to open to the interior. Sort of like an airlock on a spacecraft. Having an arctic entrance to a cabin is a common practice for those living in cold climates.

Dennis utilized the sheets of 4 × 8 feet plywood to the fullest extent, not wasting an inch. He had it well insulated. For lighting, they used one kerosene pressurized lamp, which hung in the center of the main room. There were two small bedrooms to the sides of this main room. The 7" × 11" windows were placed into the walls at head height on the inside. They placed the windows at this height because with the additional height of the dwelling from the pilings, the panes were high enough, bears could not reach from the outside. The placement and size of the windows helped ensure a bear wasn't likely to break them, but it came with a drawback. There was a very limited amount of incoming light, making the rooms dim. Dennis could have flown in full-size double-paned glass, but would have been costly, and Dennis had done his best to stay within his budget.

I was busy taking movies of all this when Jill called me, "Duane, I made something for your rifle. It's a bearskin case," then holds it up to give me, but I asked Dennis to work the camera so Jill and I can be in this presentation. I asked Jill to tell me about her work and a bit about this nice piece of work.

Jill presenting me the bear rifle case

With me showing the bear case

"The hide comes from a big old bear. You can see some white hair in it. The closing flap has bear tooth for a button."

"That is great. I thank you very much, Jill." It was like a great presentation with her handing it to me as I am in my fanciest dressed in my raccoon hat and buckskin jacket.

The boys' sled

Jill's sled

Dennis's trapping sled

We moved on to see what else they had made and took movies of the dog sleds and a sled the boys used on a hill nearby. Jill had a regular size freighting sled. Dennis's sled for trapping pulled by one very big dog on a winding trail, he said.

Shed with tanning vat and water purification system

The water filtration system

Then their water purification system and tanning vat in a small storage building and other things outside before being shown the inside of the small house.

Wood cook stove with stovepipe oven

For heating and cooking, they used a wood stove just from the center of their dwelling. A stove made for traveling light and even for living in a tent. The stove was about three feet by fourteen inches and above the floor one foot. The flat cooking surface was only two feet high, making the stove close to the floor. Above the stove was a stove pipe oven; it is set horizontally and fitted between the sections of stove pipe for convenience (see the photo). The oven had a temperature gauge on the round door to assist with backing. The temperatures of the stove pipe oven set by increasing or decreasing the incoming draft on the stove's door accordingly.

Jill had made their young son's educational board games. She put a lot of time and effort into designing and creating material that would help them meet their educational needs. These board games were not simple; they were detailed and well planned. She was very dedicated to challenging and learn how to problem solve tasks presented to them. I recall one game in particular that incorporated geographical locations on a map of the earth, including continents, countries, and states. These board games were not simple. The board games were detailed and well thought through. By that reasoning, the games were a challenge to their brains in how to solve the tasks presented to them.

One of the boys was an artist with watercolors. I believe it was Stormy. Jill told me after she was finished explaining to me about the educational board games, "Stormy has something for you to see."

"Okay, young man, what do you have to show me?"

"A picture I made. Here I will show you." He showed me a picture of a bear he had colored. It wasn't just any bear either; it was a field-dressed, dead bear.

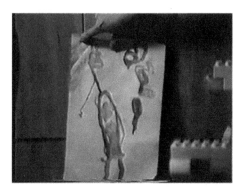

Blue water coloring of a bear's anatomy

He pointed out the internal organs—detailed and accurate. His drawing looked like a medical anatomy diagram found in most doctors' offices. As he began explaining things, his voice shook, almost like a stutter, but it was just shaky with nerves. He was enunciating every word clearly, proud to share with me what he had learned.

The following quote is exactly the way Stormy spoke; the dashes indicate his pauses. I was impressed by the way he explained his coloring to me. I shall never forget.

"This—is the—Heart—this—is the—lungs—this—is the bear's—throat, and windpipe. That—is the liver. These are—the kidneys. That big squiggly part—is his intestines. That is the bear's—small stomach. That is—his big stomach and the bone—structure."

"*Wow!*" I said. "Very well, good job. That's different, how did he ever come up with that, Jill?" I asked.

Mind you, Stormy was only a toddler at this time.

Jill explained, "We butchered a bear not long ago, and while we were cutting it up, he was very intrigued, asking all kinds of questions. He remembered everything, but we didn't realize it until he painted this picture."

Jill had both Shaun and Stormy enrolled in a homeschooling program from early on in their homesteading journey. Jill had explained to me they had a strict rule about their education, daily assignments completed before anything else the boys wanted or needed to do. No set hours for learning, but once they finished their homework, the day was theirs. So they were quick and eager to get it done. Shaun and Stormy excelled in their education, graduating much earlier than their peers enrolled in public schools, and with highest grades.

"Duane, it is dog chores time, so come along outside to meet the animals." On the lighter side, Jill with a smile effactually called the dogs, animals. Jill then led me to the dog lot, where she proceeded to feed three dogs. Two were theirs, one was Oliver Cameron's. (Oliver was a homesteader neighbor.) The dogs were named Buddy, Bones, and Chena. Bones belonged to Oliver; he was being taken care of by the Hannans while Oliver was in town away from his homestead. Oliver's dwelling and homestead were nearby Jill's.

Jill's dwelling was still in the construction stage, but it was close to being ready for her. She would need to spend five months a year for the next five years' homesteading requirements, but her time living on her homestead wouldn't count until she began living in the dwelling. Jill's required time was longer than mine because she was not a veteran.

A white dog named Buddy

An old dog named Bones

Elkhound named Chena

We walked a short distance and up a slight incline to where the dogs were staked separated from each other. These dogs were three happy jumping dogs, waiting for attention and food. I had come to know Buddy while Sam Connors lived close to my dugout. I was amazed at how much he had grown since I last saw him. "Wow! Is that Buddy? You got from Sam Conner, right? He sure has gotten big?"

"Yup, sure is."

Jill pointed to one of her dogs and introduced me to Chena. She went to explain to me how Chena was a tunneler and had a long tunnel in the ground, in much the same way wolves do. Chena was no wolf; however, she was part elkhound. She was a very intelligent dog, responding well to the commands and demands put on her like a sled dog.

Their dogs were overjoyed to see us, and it was clear none had a mean bone in their body. The Hannans were good to their dogs, and it showed.

In all my travels, I have seen many dogs, both mistreated as well as those loved and cherished. I have no problem recognizing the look of mistreatment in a dog's facial expressions. Here with the Hannans, it was clear by the affectionate way these dogs behaved toward the masters they loved and who loved them.

The earthen refrigerator

After the dogs had been cared for and fed, we moved back to the house where Dennis showed me an earthen hillside cooler he had near his cabin that they used as a refrigerator. For the lack of lumber, he constructed a lot of things with small peeled logs. This cooler was built with peeled small fencepost-sized logs and its door of even smaller logs. In front of this door was what is known as a bear board. A bear board is a spiked nailed, with the protruding, extended sharp ends up, a welcome mat so to speak.

The earthen cellar

Together the Hannans were eager to show me an even larger earthen cellar storage structure dug into a high steep tree and moss-covered dune. That has to have formed millions of years ago when the area was a desert. The excavated hillside–built structure was timbered, walled by peeled spruce poles; it even had a window and could be used as a livable shelter if the need arose—as if in the case of their main dwelling being burned down. We gathered inside so I could get a closer look. This structure was used instead as a standing cache and was much more secure.

Once we completed the tour of the storage structure, Jill took me to see their clothesline strung from tree to tree. It was not an ordinary line, but a dual season clothesline. That set up had an upper line and a lower line, the higher line used in the winter and the lower in the summer.

How could a winter line be different from a summer line? Well because the snow is not shoveled but packed and walked on until it melts in the spring. Unlike in towns, paths are not shoveled but packed forming solid frozen sidewalk-type paths for all winter.

We continued my tour of the homestead by walking down a path that leads us through a young forest of poplar trees and birch mix. The trees' largest diameters were about eight inches. That was a well-used path and eventually opened up clear of trees, and there in front of me stood a larger than a normal cache that looked like a one room cabin on stilts. Again, this building was also made entirely from snuggly fitted small and neatly peeled spruce poles.

The big cache

Dennis, in seeing I was impressed, said, "We were tired of having three to four small caches, so we built this big one."

This cache was held up by four posts. The floor was ten feet above the ground. It was seven feet wide by ten feet long, and the walls were six feet high. A wooden ladder was used to reach the door to the cache. The pole supporting the storage unit had wrapped around steel plating nailed to them to prevent climbing critters, such as wolverine, from reaching their goods. If a wolverine found a way in, it would be a disaster. Not only would they be destructive but would leave a most horrible stink on everything. On the posts supporting this cache were nailed on with wrap around steel plating to prevent any climbing critters like even a wolverine from getting in their stuff.

As I examined the posts, I could see where a grizzly bear had left its teeth and claw marks in an attempt to break in. It had stood on its hind feet, reaching the underside of the cache, leaving its trademark carved into the logs. "We have a need to carry big guns out here," Dennis told me.

They weren't done showing me their craftsmanship. We left the cache and wandered over to another structure, this one two stories tall. It had an open-air lean-to shed attached to one side. This building Dennis called the Barn, which had lots of room for tools and such. In the lean-to, there were stacks of firewood stored. They had explained to me the wood kept out there was for emergency purposes, such as if something were to happen to either parent or, worse case, both.

Jill's earthen mound

Entries to the hole in the ground

Located about eighty feet to the east of the barn, I noticed a large mound of rounded earth that reminded me of a hobbit's home. This uniquely earthen home, Dennis affectional called Jill's Hole in the Ground and laughed. The mound was seeded with lawn grass and had an extended rectangular entrance covered by earth. The entrance was narrow and had steps leading down to a four-foot long hallway. It was an excellent organic arctic entryway. The door leading into the home opened inward. I noticed they had installed a four-inch square gun port hatch in the door, which could open from the inside of the door. Upon examining the inside of the door, I saw they had constructed it to hold a cross beam, which would act as a brace keeping the bear from smashing the door.

The Hannan family treated my visit like I was a celebrity and never once left my side or out of earshot; it was now time to show and tell. But that was the way it was living in the wilderness without seeing anyone for months or years on end. This experience is something a city dweller or even a person living in a rural area with a mailbox never has experienced.

Jill and the boys led me inside all the while explaining everything, from the excavation using shovels and buckets used to move the soil. The cutting and dragging of the hundreds of dry burned trees, the time it took to peel the spruce poles. They were continually taking turns in filling me in on the details. Everyone had a role in building this earthen home.

Inside earthen home window

Counter shelves

Ceiling

To my immediate amazement, I had walked into a big bright-lit shiny room. Here's where it gets interesting. Jill was smiling at my reaction and let me look around in ah. At first, I wasn't saying anything. I was scanning the whole room from end to end and top to bottom. The window gave a gorgeous view of the land to the northwest, overlooking Dead Fish Lake located a short distance away. "I have to tell you, you all have done an amazing job. Excellent craftsmanship, I can see a lot of time has gone into building this."

The brilliant rays of sunshine were filtering in through a wide bay window to the left of where I was standing. I saw a six-foot wide window by three feet installed in the center of the wall. The bottom of the window was about ten inches above a kitchen counter. The floor was white and bright from the reflective rays of light, covered by some hardened material. Beneath the floor's hard surface, Dennis had explained to me, was a two-inch blue foam board used as a vapor barrier; it also served as insulation separating the floor from the cool sandy earth beneath it.

The room's side walls were built in sections beginning with the lower section being three-foot high, then each section after that angled more until the walls became the roof. You might say in the fashion that of an igloo. The other two walls were built straight up like a normal wall.

The main living room's space was about twelve feet by eighteen feet. The ceiling's height was not all that high, but just enough so that my head cleared the support beams that held the roof from collapsing. Dennis and Jill were not as tall as me, so it was just right for them.

The entire interior of the home had been waterproofed, preventing any possible water seepage from the ground, or leaks from heavy rains. Three of the walls from waist-high to the apex where the sloped roof met were made from smaller peeled spruce poles, placed in an upright position.

To the left of the entrance of the main room was the wood stove. The stove's legs stood on a heat-resistant board, with an additional board shielding the wood wall behind it. Where the stove's pipe went through the ceiling, there was a gasoline can with a stovepipe hole on each end for the stovepipe. The stovepipe-modified gas can complete with a second smaller placed inside, and then sand-filled in the double cans. That acted as an insulation system, which prevented the transfer of heat to any of the roof's combustible materials.

This system makes for a safe chimney in the case of a runaway chimney fire. Chimney fires are the main causes of house fires.

There was a sheet of heavy gauge steel on the top of the roof around the stoves chimney top, to protect the sod rooftop from any hot ash.

To my immediate right with my back toward the entry door was a peeled spruce pole wall from the floor to the ceiling, crossing the room. There were two door openings along this wall, with curtains hung instead of wood doors. They used these rooms as bedrooms, the master's bedroom and the bedroom with bunk beds for the boys.

The Hannans had poured many hours into drawknife peeling of the countless spruce poles that made up this building. Not only had the poles been skinned by a drawknife, and fitted, but they were decorative by leaving parts of the brown cambium layer on the poles. Jill's Alaskan Hobbit Home was an earthen home. Living in an earthen home is wise, economical on heating and cooling.

View of window from the outside

After they were done showing me around their home dwelling, we returned outside so that I could see the wide window from the front of the home. Jill had planted a small but lush garden planted in front of this window, and it was flourishing from the fertile soil. Dennis had installed a bear-proof log shutter for the window, which could be swung up to protect the window when the house was left unattended.

Dennis collected water from the lake but before transporting screened it. Filling jugs using their two dogs to pack the water back home for further cleaning it with an elaborate water purification system. This system consisting of a series of five-gallon buckets with round cutouts in the bottoms of the buckets, and the holes filled with compressed sponges. The water passed through three stages of filtration, before being stored in large containers housed in a secured outbuilding. Parasites were the main reason for purifying the water. Pure water is a luxury society often taken for granted, but out in the wilderness, it is a matter of life or death and is guaranteed with purposeful and careful preparation.

The Hannans preferred the taste of lake water versus rainwater and used rainwater for other purposes.

Another source of water in the early spring before the rains came, they tapped water from birch trees for drinking.

We had completed my tour of the Hannans' homestead, so they lead me down a path to their neighbor's place, Oliver Cameron. Oliver had left his home bear-proofed while he was visiting Fairbanks, so I was given a limited tour around the homestead. Oliver's cache was about twenty feet from his window of similar in size and materials as the Hannans.

Front of Oliver's underground home

Oliver lived in a hole in the ground, a term of endearment we have for earthen homes. Oliver's place was well camouflaged and sheltered by the trees and brush of the forest. It was undetectable from the air and hidden from view of the nearby lake. He hadn't wanted his home out in the open like both Dennis's and Jill's. Should a wildfire ever occur in this area, Oliver and his home would be trapped. It was a risk some like him were willing to take to stay safe out of sight of the pirates. Living out in the wilderness doesn't always bring protection from the bad guys. It's not uncommon for remote homes to be robbed and pillaged of what goods they hold while the owners are away. The items stolen might not be of value to anyone, but the owner living in the wilderness makes belongings more likely irreplaceable.

In walking around Oliver's home, I did not see an outhouse, so I asked Dennis, "Dennis, where is his outhouse?"

Dennis and Jill looked at each other, then turned and looked at a grass-constructed outhouse.

"You're kidding me, right?"

"Nope! That is his outhouse like none other," Jill made the comment. "Oliver is original."

I have seen countless of outhouses in my day, but never one like Oliver's. His toilet was a small grass hut, big enough for use, with no extra space. Oliver had constructed a wooden fence like the frame and thatched long bear grass for the walls and roof. Although it was flimsy, it was buried deep in the woods, protected from winds and driving rain. The grass-thatched covering kept the rain that reached it from leaking inside. Inside, there was a hole in the ground, meaning the user would have to crouch over and hover. That was enough visuals for me; it was time to move on.

The day had been very interesting, but it was now time to walk back to their first home. It had been a long day, but a woman's work is never-ending. Jill fixed a fine supper fit for the gods. The pressurized lamp was making a hissing sound while we visited. After supper was eaten, Dennis went outside to his cooler, grabbed an otter hide he had been tanning, and brought it inside. Dennis dampened the leather and proceeded to stretch the stiffness from it by pulling it with his hands, limbering the leather.

Dennis explained that Jill wants to experiment in making waterproof mukluks for him. That is why the otter hide.

He then, while sitting, placed an upright board with a secured flat base on the floor, which he held by his feet and closed knees tightly. Both the top six-inch horizontal and the first vertical eight inches on the opposite side, the edges are sharpened. That he explained to be a "breaker board." This top end while sitting was chest height. With the raw side of the otter's pelt now up against the sharp vertical edge of the breaker board and using both hands to grip, one hand on each end of the long hide proceeds to pull tightly rapidly directly back and forth several times, making an abrasive rubbing noise continuing until the completion of the whole hide.

Rubbing the hide in this manner causes the leather pores to break down, releasing the natural oils contained in the cells of the leather, thus the name breaker board. Next, he washed the hide rinsing the oils out and let it dry overnight.

In the days to follow, Dennis would complete the tanning by rubbing in the otter's smashed brain matter. The brain contained acid and needed for the electrical thought process of every being. The smashed-up brain from the animal is enough to tan the hide. Battery acid sometimes is used as a substitute instead of or enough brain matter, but this is not my area of expertise. Instead, I would leave the usage of battery acid to the professionals. Eventually, the leather becomes supple and ready for making garments whatever the fur is by matching the colors of other furs, not by dying the fur color, at least here in Alaska.

The making of garments, hats, beaver over mitts, mittens, or marten, and lynx shawls is Jill's department whether for home use or to be sold for extra income in a tourist shop. Special thread and the use of a needle made just for leather. A leather needle is not round but has three sides to it, making the leather needle's hole it made easier to pull the thread through.

All homemade fur garments made by Alaskans sold in the tourist shops are high in value. So look for the label made in Alaska. (Made in China or Alaska.) Here is but one example I saw in the summer of 1984, a queen-size bed blanket of matching color beaver pelts cut in octagons, stitched together without a backing, sells for $4,500 at a tourist shop near Kenai, Alaska. When you shop for fur garments in Alaska, bring money.

Soon after Dennis had washed the otter hide, we heard, "Okay, I have supper ready, come and get it!" Until then, I had not thought of food, but I woofed it down all the same. Supper consisted of baked potatoes and a plate or two of baked beans with sweet molasses on them. After which we took turns telling stories, mostly of the things the Hannans had done to achieve what they have done.

It was now the boy's bedtime. Stormy and Shaun, one by one, said to me, "Good night, Duane," to which in turn I said to each of them good night. That part of saying a good night was like the Walton family exchanging their good nights to each other one at a time and back one at a time. Jill and the boys went to their room, and I could hear them saying their prayers together with their mom.

The three of us stayed up continuing our visiting until Jill reminded us we had a long day tomorrow, and we should call it a night. Then once again, it was telling each other good night using our names back and forth. There was no simple saying of "good night."

In the morning, at eight thirty, Jill made a gut-filling breakfast of biscuits and gravy. I asked Jill, "When did you make the biscuits?"

"Last night, after we had said our good nights."

"Man! I didn't hear a thing, you must have been very quiet."

"Oh, Duane, if I was making any noise, you're snoring covered that."

The boy's just laughed, and Dennis smiled, followed by me saying, "Umm, that was sure was good."

We were soon interrupted by the loud roaring engine of a plane buzzing over our heads. Jill shouted to me, "It's my dad. He said he was coming today, but I didn't know he'd be here so early."

We ran to the lake, not wanting to miss the plane that we knew wouldn't stick around long before it headed back to town. Dennis had heard the plane before we did and was well ahead of us with the outgoing mail bag.

I was bringing up the rear in case a bear attacked us from behind, one can never be too careful out here. But in all reality, I was the last dog falling behind; my age was showing. I was closing in on the lake when I heard the plane take back up into the air and head off to the north. Dennis had received a bag of mail and handed the pilot the outgoing mail. That was quick.

Chuck looking airsick

When I caught up, Dennis was moving to higher ground with the luggage and supplies the plane had brought. Jill's father was still standing on the shoreline, not moving, holding one hand to his belly and looking pale.

Jill introduced us. "Dad, this is Duane Ose, and, Duane, this is my dad, Chuck Phillips from Eugene, Oregon. Dad has made plans to be here for about a month."

"It's a pleasure to meet you, Chuck. Jill has told me a lot about you."

Jill was hugging him with one arm around his waist gently while running her other hand to him as it was very evident to all of us he was recovering from motion sickness.

I assured Chuck by telling him, "You will be feeling better in a few minutes, take your time."

Chuck gradually recovered from the flight in time, then we together made our way back to Dennis's place. Chuck was looking from side to side as he walked with the boys in the lead. The rest of us were carrying the things that came in with Chuck.

A family photo

I took the time to film the whole family in front of their wood shed and storage building.

Once we settled in the cabin, we stayed up late swapping stories. It didn't take for me to realize what a great father Jill had. I began to look forward to working with him while he was out here. We already had some things planned for in the days to come. Chuck's knee would get plenty of exercise during his twenty-seven-day stay. Oh ya, Chuck Philips would have had the experience of a lifetime after his time up here.

Thirty days previous to his trip to visit the Hannans, Chuck, had microscopic knee surgery. He planned to stay out on the homestead until the third of September. It wasn't long before Chuck earned a nickname from us. You have guessed it, Wounded Knee.

Chuck had brought an abundant amount of goodies with him, and the next morning Jill treated us to a meal of hash browns, eggs, biscuits, and gravy.

After the hardy breakfast, Dennis and I headed back to the trailhead on Long Lake, where he had planned to see me off as I headed home. Jokingly, I turned to Dennis and said, "You might have to take me by hand and show me how to get back to my bridge on Levi Lake."

Since Dennis having been on the ridgeline several times before, he knew the way best, saving me from exploring and marking the route. Dennis helped me mark the trail with the red roll of survey tape that I had in my pocket specifically to mark it on my way back home. In marking the trail, we kept inline, keeping it straight by tying flagging spaced apart enough so that we could see at all times three flags for alinement, as seeing only two flags at a time would not assure us of having a straight trail. This method made it easy to keep the trail straight. The woods and undergrowth were extremely thick, and my engineering experience in road building came in handy.

CHAPTER 14

Ridgeline Trail

When building roads or even trails without the use of heavy earth-moving equipment, the rule is to follow the terrain and keep out of the wetlands. This section of the trail was densely forested, making it difficult to see the terrain that was on a long wide ridge. We only had to keep on top and follow the highest part of the terrain. Thankfully, Dennis had come to know this ridge quite well early on. This trail would be an ATV trail from the east end of the newly built eighty-foot bridge, and the trailhead at Long Lake. The Ridgeline Trail would be a link, making it easier and a faster travel time between Dead Fish Lake and Ose Mountain.

We're working together, neighbors for improving our community, far removed from any other society of rules or village ardencies but more as a remote "township" living off the grid. The board that met for being united, resolving any issues that should arise involving our common needs and formed by we the people for the people. We agreed that all labor, food, tools, fuel, machines, ammo is to be donated and shared by we the people, which is a small form of a volunteer governing local society for a joint cause.

Since I had the chainsaw with the experience in falling trees, I went ahead, cutting down all the larger trees, cutting the deadfalls into short lengths, making the wood easy to toss aside as we moved forward and all the while making a four-foot wide trail. Jill used the smaller lopping shears cutting the nuisance stuff, of which chainsaws

do not react well. A rotating chain can easily break or be thrown off
the bar by a small twig.

Chuck and Dennis clearing trail

It was rather enjoyable working as a team, each knowing what
to do, with no questions asked. Jill was good with the long handled
shear. Her work saved us a lot of bend over finish work and rework.
Even Wounded Knee moved like there was nothing wrong with his
knee. Shaun and Stormy were having fun tossing cut and fallen dead
material to the sides.

Jill asks us a dumb question about midway into the trail cutting
process. "Is there anyone interested in lunch?" Wounded Knee
without hesitation lowered himself to the ground, curled up, "You
bet." The rest of us remained standing. Our hands held our open
canteens while the tools laid on the ground.

Me eating peach cobbler

Jill approached me and held before my face an uncovered cake pan of peach cobbler, with a long ladle. I drooled for a moment, forgetting about sharing. I was a pig. I then without thinking had quickly eaten a row and a half of the pre-sliced cobbler before I had realized others were looking at me strangely. They were politely waiting, and I said that was good as I handed the cake pan back to Jill. Jill was blushingly smiling and giggling.

Chuck was holding the pan now as everyone else was diving in, eating directly from the cake pan. When suddenly, Chuck reaches into the pan, then with this thumb and forefinger extracted a short, small wiggly green worm. Chuck looks up the tree branches overhead. "Anyone want some protein with their cobbler?"

Chuck looking up in tree to where a tree worm fell from

A leaf worm had dropped into the pan. The much-welcomed lunchbreak was over, and we went back to work with renewed vigor.

Beneath this wide ridge of green mossy vegetation are found windblown sand and volcanic ash. Windstorms billions of years ago formed ridges like the drifting sands of deserts. That was once an arid desert region and remains reality aired yet today but green. The first vegetation was moss allowing the other plants to grow. Over times, volcanic ash fell from the stratosphere. The volcanic ash came from the countless, once violent, and now extinct, dormant. Alaska is known for its past and present volcanic activity.

The ash is gray in color, crystalline, and abrasive made of superheated stone. This ash covered Alaska's lands to varying depths from inches to hundreds of feet. After billions of hot tropical years, the earth cooled. The ashen land was then covered during the cooling times four times during the last ten thousand years by deep snows up to thousands of feet deep, resulting in four ice ages of the packed snow that turned into ice with the century periods of warm weather, and in between the centuries of the cold centuries creating the ice fields we know as glaciers. The last reaching as far south as the northern part of the contiguous lower 48 states before receding. Ice fields are melting and forming yet today.

My greater question is, what drastic transformation earth changes might occur next?

Here in volcanic Alaska, some glaciers had, through time, been covered by several feet of ash that had insulated them, slowing or even stopping in parts the thawing process. On this ridge that we were cutting a trail, I discovered sinkholes in different areas. Upon investigating by digging down into them beyond the fallen-in trees and rotted vegetation, I found gray volcanic ash. This gray ash covered green ice, a glacier. Green ice is ice that contains no oxygen, which is why the color green. Green ice can be several feet to hundreds of feet thick. When green ice is found trapped buried beneath any soil, it is called a pingle. A pingle was once part of a melting, living, moving glacier.

The covering of this ice by ash perhaps occurred thousands of years ago, or more likely as recently as ten thousand years during the last of the four known ice ages. I found this trail project ongoing expanding sinkholes the same as I have often found in other locations. I have even collected drinking water from the green-colored ice. That means I have drunk water that was snow compressed and formed into the ice of perhaps ten or more thousands of years ago.

The sinkholes on this trail we wisely detoured. In this area, sinkholes were occurring due to the heat sink effect down to the ice because of the gradual lack of the insulating surface covering by denning animals.

These slow-growing, expanding sink holes were becoming larger each year clogged with fallen-in full-grown trees and surface material. During heavy rainstorms, the rainwater would be funneled into and down these sinkholes, aiding in thawing the pingle deep below. Sinkholes sometimes are used by a bear or bears in which to hibernate during the long winter months.

I will further add that these sinkholes are at the top of the long ridge. But in one location, I found a waterway, which encouraged a growing sinkhole by taking in a large area of rainwater.

I love earth sciences.

Mind you, besides these detours around the sinkholes, we also saved some of the better trees by bypassing them as well.

It had been a long working day when we called it a day and headed back to our homes. The longest part completed and the hard part, tomorrow's work would complete the trail.

Back now in the dugout was another life for me to live. Not only in doing my cooking, but I was also cooking for the bears mostly every morning and evening. I was never alone as it seems. There were the bear visits, yard work, and water to collect from the cool fresh spring, and the conversations on the CB. While at home, I would leave the CB turned on, Jill would give me wake up calls at eight thirty like a timely alarm and a CB visit in the evenings.

While not transmitting the CB, leaving it on was not using much battery power, so it was little concern.

Also, I was enjoying reading of the mail that was air-dropped at the Hannans at a more regular basis now, and they kindly delivered it to me at the trailhead or brought all the way to the dugout at times.

The second day of trail work, Jill awoke me by calling me on the CB at eight thirty, and said, "Duane, its wake-e-wake-e time."

"Hello, Muskeg Momma, I was just fixing the pancakes."

"Sure you are, Duane. I am calling to let you know the men are headed out."

"Okay, I'll be there in a short, short." I gulped down the pancakes, locked the door, hooked up the trailer, then put in my earth-moving tools and drove down.

Building this end of the ridgeline trail was a whole lot easier, and by 1:00 p.m., Chuck, Dennis, and I had completed it. That made for the first time that I could drive the ATV to the trailhead. Chuck and Dennis canoed back to the Hannan homesteads.

Earlier in the days of walking this trail, I knew I would need to do some earth work on the hill coming up from the Long Lake trailhead to the top of the ridge. For this, I had in my trailer an ax, shovel, and a pick ax. This section had a sharp steep drop-off at the high end dropping down to the lake. So it was a simple matter of chopping the ground cover. The ground had no stones, not even sand, only clay over ash under the mosses. I shoveled the chopped root system, and ash grading the material downhill, shaping it for a more gradual slope. That made the trail safe and usable for the ATV to travel both ways.

After which, I called it a day and drove home to see what the bears had been up to today. But instead, after my return to my dugout, I saw I had a shoeless, two-legged visitor that left the usual calling card a length of firewood on my path near the outhouse. I was not alone nor was I in fear. I had come to know the Hairy Ones, and they showed their trust in me, although they remained, shyly toyed with me.

CHAPTER 15

Time to Work, Time to Visit

This year, goals had been completed, with more yet to be reached.

1. The completion of the smoke house.
2. Locating trees to girdle for drying them while they were left to stand to be ready for the first of the house logs.
3. The cutting of two more trails.
4. Lastly, to excavate the walkout basement for the house.

These four unfinished goals had to be done before the snowy mountain passes closed to drive safely back down the Alaskan-Canadian Highway. To achieve those four remaining goals, I had to push myself because time was running out for this season.

The building of the smokehouse has become a fill in the project and seems now to be never-ending. For many reasons that this project has slowed was that the chainsaw's bars were wearing the kerfs wider. The kerf is the grove that the chain is held in close tolerance, keeping the chain from moving side-to-side as it rotates on the bar. Also, the chain's guide links were wearing narrowly thin for the bar's widening kerf as well, compounding the problem of a wobbling, clogging, slow-cutting chain.

It was not a problem in the sharpening of the chains. But the chain's links were being stretched to their limits. These chains were about to break apart during the saw's running operation, to fly wildly about, possibly causing an injury.

To adjust the bar's kerfs, I had no closing or sizing tool to close the kerf to the width needed, so I improvised by using a trusty hand tool called a vise grip—carefully adjusting the clinching process of the vise grip so as not to close the kerf more than was needed, or worse, to break the bar's kerf.

I was cautiously sawing lumber and dealing with a worn out bar and chains. Luckily I had seen this problem developing and had sent a request to my brother Mike in Redwood Falls, Minnesota, for new bars, chains, and drive sprockets. It made my day when the parts arrived. I then quickly finished sawing the lumber for the rafters, roof, and the four-foot wide door. Then even boards for the porch and doorstep. Thank you, my brother, Mike.

At the time, I had only had poly sheeting to cover, waterproof the roof boards. Then I weighed the poly sheeting down with saw log slabs until in the future I'd have better roofing material. I had installed the heating stove, its chimney at which point this then finished the smokehouse. The interior would be insulated and finished next year, but for now, I had a safe, dry place to store my ATV and supplies.

The timing of closing in the smokehouse could not have been better. Because tonight on Trapline Chatter, Wednesday, August 19, Oliver Cameron messaged that he was arriving at Dead Fish Lake before noon tomorrow. After the message, I called on the CB and Dennis agreed to pick me up at the long lake trailhead early in the morning. That way we all could be there when Oliver arrived. That then sent me scrambling to get several letters written and ready before morning. Note: To the certain people who are reading this, I thank you for your letters. I dang near got writer's cramps that night.

In the morning, I drove to all the way to where Dennis awaited me without incident. We loaded the canoe and paddled our way to Denise's trailhead. From there, we walked to Dennis's place to meet up with Jill and the boys. Then quickly we walked to Dead Fish Lake, arriving just in time.

The plane was just landing as we approached the shoreline of Dead Fish Lake. It was a quick disembarkation of Oliver with his bags. Then we handed the pilot our mail including my recent VHS tapes. Before the plane's engine had a chance to cool, the plane was back in the air.

While in town, Oliver had stopped in at KJNP of North Pole and had picked up all the letters that had been sent there and read to us. "Thank you, Oliver, that was good of you."

Oliver in Jill's home

That was the first time Oliver and I met in person. Oliver was a tall, lean man, clean shaven, age sixty-five, who wore a felt black tall pointy hat that had a wide flattened rim with no shape. The hat was not fancy but of quality material that kept the sun out of his eyes, and to shed the rain. He wore no glasses, but only for reading or close work. Oliver was stone-deaf, and as I talked, he watched my lips. I had to almost yell the words, speaking slowly and distinctly each word.

He had a large pronounced adjustable hearing aid sticking out of one ear. Oliver had lost his hearing during WWII when he was a gunner on a bomber. He and I had been talking to each other previously most every night on the CB radio. While talking to the CB, Oliver would plug in the CB speaker wire into his hearing aid. That made it easier to converse on the CB than in person. Talking to Oliver in person, I limited my talking to him, but instead, I pointed at things. He would understand and would explain in detail what he wished me to know. When I did talk to him, he had no qualms of cupping a hand to his ear and lean into my voice.

Oliver had no teeth and gummed his food, which was mush or pre-ground before he swallowed it. There were no three square meals a day for him. But he ate a small amount many times a day because of his small stomach. However, he did love to eat butter. While visiting Jill's place at one time, I saw Oliver eat one pound of butter of Jill's, one spoonful at a time as I would eat ice cream and about as fast. Oliver ate nothing else with it, only the one pound of butter. I wondered why, but I did not ask. I am sure that by Oliver eating in one setting, a whole pound of butter of the Hannans, was frustrating for Jill, knowing supplies sometimes to be at six-month intervals.

I had my ways, and Oliver had his ways, but we still respected one another. The one thing I disagreed with was the way he viewed dogs. I told him right out that I disagreed. He was as adamant in his way as I was in my way. Oliver believed dogs and all animals were to serve man. Also, they had no soul and would not be admitted into heaven. Oliver explained a dog was to obey commands by disciplining, not by affection or rewards. A dog was fed only to be fueled to be healthy enough to serve him.

Normally when Oliver flies into town, he routinely shoots his dog, killing the dog, dumping it in the lake at the last minute before getting on the plane to Fairbanks. If, as he had done in the past, he would have had the time, he skins the dog and dries the hide, tanning it. Then before leaving Fairbanks, he would go to the animal shelter and buy a new young dog to bring home.

Oliver told me in detail why not just any dog would do, but only one with patches over the eyebrows. A dog with patches over the eyebrows to Oliver meant that it was a smart dog at least in his way of thinking or perhaps the experience he has had with many dogs.

It got so the animal shelter in Fairbanks cringed every time Oliver stopped in to buy a dog or adopted one, for the people at the animal shelters figured out what Oliver was doing with the dogs. Oliver did always pay for the veteran-required shots the dog had received.

This time that Oliver was to make a trip to town, and after a great amount of pleading by the Hannans, Oliver let the Hannans feed and care for Bones. Bones, as it turned out, was Oliver's next to the last dog and was well trained. Bones became old in the years following, and Oliver bought a new dog and named him Pack.

Oliver had eaten most of his previous dogs when they became old and were no longer of any use to him. His dogs were always given a name, not a real pet's kind of a name but only for the purpose of calling out the distinct commands, such as Pack? Pack's name was with the intent of being used for packing. Pack carried in the saddle packs, everything needed for an extended hike. In time, he shot Pack, too, in one of the years to follow. Oliver himself had become frail and ill. He decided to leave his homestead to live with others that would tend to his needs and left his property to his daughter, who lives in California.

Oliver had since passed on, so I wonder if he was surprised to find dogs on another side.

After a hot meal, Dennis brought me back to the trailhead that same day, and I drove on home feed Mr. Bear and called it a day.

The next day, Friday, the 21st of August, the Hannans and Wounded Knee, Chuck Phillips, came to spend the next five days with me. That was why previously I had stated the smokehouse finished in time. Suddenly it was no longer a smokehouse; it now had become a guest house, which the Hannans slept in, and Chuck slept on the lower bunk in the dugout.

I was the cook that night and made up a kettle of beef stew. The next morning, Jill took over the cooking. We had a filling breakfast and that night a hearty supper. But not until we worked as a whole group cleaning up and salvaging all of Sam Connor's two camps that he had left in disarray. One item that I have of his is a guitar that he had left out in the weather to ruin and rot. That cleanup of his camps took us all day; it was our nature to have the wilderness restored even though no one else would ever know the mess he had left behind or see it.

The third day, Dennis and I spent a long day marking a trail route to Wien Lake, which was a difficult thing to do and only was able to mark out about three and three-fourth miles, not even half ways for future cutting. While we were doing this, Chuck and Jill were busy working back at the dugout on other things like getting water for drinking, cooking, yard cleaning, and splitting cooking wood.

We watched a VHS movie during the evening, eating popcorn, visiting, and most notably of all to me during this time was, we were not visited by any of the bear, or Little People. They were most likely around, but respected us by staying back in the woods, and perhaps did not trust any strangers. That was just as well for everyone that way. I needed no more bearskin rifle cases or butchering to do.

The fourth day, we worked on the cutting of the Wien Lake trail and made over a mile. Jill had taken time that day and picked blueberries from a blueberry bog we had cut a trail nearby. That night while Chuck and I washed some clothes, Jill baked a big blueberry pie.

The fifth day, we went up to the top of the hill with the ATV and trailer, then down on a trail partway to Wien Lake's creek for a family picnic. This ATV trail to the creek, I and Larry had cut to within one mile of the creek. This rest of way we had to walk, which was a bit of a struggle for the boys and Jill. I would, in the next few days, finish cutting that trail right to the bank of the creek.

Roasting marshmallows

On that fifth day, although the extra time it took to walk down and back to the creek, it was well worth it. On film, I have the event all recorded. Jill had brought marshmallows. The boys enjoyed in making a small safe fire roast the marshmallows on the shore of the creek. That was a great photo op for me, seeing a good time by all. Next, it was down on the gravel bars, and for the first time in the boy's lives they held stones in their hands and, as you could imagine right away, began tossing them into the water. Most notably when the boys tossed the stones, they tossed them starting with their hands by their ears. It was an awkward way of tossing stones. I could clearly see they never tossed any small stones before. At their homestead on Dead Fish Lake, there are no stones of any kind to toss.

Jill and Chena

Chena, their favorite dog, was at Jill's side lying on a sandbar getting petted, while her and I looked on watching Shaun and Stormy tossing stones for the first time. I could plainly tell they had no idea of how to throw a stone; it was more like a pushing of the arm forward from their shoulders than opening their hand widely, releasing the stone. Not overhand or underhand or sidearm, but a push. The stones did not travel far. I think they liked the sound of ca-plush! The splash! They had no intentions of trying to hit anything, but the water.

Shaun and Stormy tossing stones

At the end of their time here at the creek, they filled their deep pockets with stones to bring back to their home—sort of like the rocks brought back from the surface of the moon's lunar landing. After all, those stones to the boys were a big deal.

Chuck panning for gold

I had brought along a testing metal gold pan (the smaller Gold Pan used in locating gold), which Chuck and Dennis soon put to work. I watched, taking movies of this. They were doing well but never digging down deep enough to hardpan to find the real color or the heavies. The gold was inches away deeper down, but their washing and shaking was good, and they did end up having black sand in their pan. Black sand is the iron sand that indicates gold might be close. What was needed was a pick and shovel, or to move the large boulders, and explore the gravels beneath. The saying is, "Gold is where you find it!"

Chuck carves his name and date in tree

It was time to head back up the hill some three miles to Ose Mountain. While passing through the birch forest midway up the hill, Chuck took time out to carve his name at shoulder height into a ten-inch diameter white birch tree, and dated August 25, 1987 (Tuesday). From that point, the boys rode in the trailer as Chuck drove while Dennis, Jill, and I were walking behind, all the way up to the top, then down the trail to the dugout.

During this time, walking through the old birch forest, Stormy and Shaun collected tree mushrooms more than their arms could hold. Therefore, the mushrooms were placed in the trailer. The boys had as much excitement in finding mushrooms, that they were like prospectors finding gold nuggets.

At the dugout, we had a very short rest, loaded the trailer with their gear and the boys, then Chuck rode with me on the ATV the three and a half miles down to the lake. Dennis was operating the camcorder, which at one point as Chuck, and I passed the Frenchman's Cabin now near the lake while on the Honda. I heard on the VHS tape later, Dennis saying, "Here they come around the bend."

At my dock, Dennis, again with the camcorder turned on, recorded Chuck taking pictures of Denali Mountain. Dennis was also talking as he recorded (Dennis was referring to Chuck taking pictures), "He's setting the adjustments...aiming...and shoots! He got it!" Chuck could hear Dennis, and it was annoying for Chuck some, but Chuck was doing his best to get that photo the best he could for there was not enough 35-millimeter film to shoot a vast amount of shots. No wasting of the precious film as epically here in the bush.

Driving over bridge

We left the dock and I drove this time with Jill. Chuck and Dennis walked to the Long Lake's trailhead following us. Jill sat behind me on the ATV, and the boys were riding in the trailer. Dennis videoed my driving over the long eighty-foot bridge, talking slowly, clearly, and distinctly these words, "It's a beautiful day in the bush," at the same time showing Denali Mountain in all its splendid glory and then panning back to me, saying, "Keep it between the edges of the bridge, Duane."

While sitting behind me, Jill was at no loss for words. We talked all the way to the trailhead.

Loading canoe

Jill fills my canteen

At the trailhead of Long Lake, we loaded the canoe that looked small with three adults, two youngsters, Chena, and backpacks. The water was calm as glass thankfully. Before Jill climbed in, she refilled my canteen. Before Dennis shoved the canoe into the deeper water, I tried to raise Oliver on the handheld CB to let him know the Hannans were on their way back. But there was no response, all I could hear static, so we figured he was outdoors feeding Pack and the Hannans' other dog.

It was a clear, beautiful late afternoon all the while recording, and I had no problem in hearing them talking to me some distance from shore. We were saying to each other our goodbyes. "Goodbye, Duane," Shawn said.

"Goodbye, Shawn."

"Goodbye, Duane," Stormy said.

"Goodbye Stormy."

"Goodbye, Duane," Dennis said.

"Goodbye, Dennis," I said.

"Goodbye, Duane," Chuck said.

"Goodbye, Chuck."

"Goodbye, Duane," Jill said.

"Goodbye, Jill." The last thing I heard as they were long ways from me was Jill saying, "I'll call you tonight."

I replied, "The water is about eight inches from coming inside the canoe, be careful now, and have a safe trip."

Hannans in canoe

I held my camera, leaving it turned on, with them in the center of the viewfinder while I talked to myself until they paddled almost out of sight. I was watching close friends leaving with the magnificent, bright, shining Denali Mountain to their front. It was some difficult moments of time knowing we would not be seeing each other again for perhaps a year.

In no time, I was back up on Ose Mountain and parked overlooking my dugout. Then suddenly without warning, a strange thing happened to me. For the first time in my life, the very instant I turned off the 350cc Honda, I had not prepared for what was happening.

The last five days and nights, I had living, breathing, talking interaction with five people. All that ended the very split second the Honda's engine was turned off. The space around me was of total silence, not even a rustle of windblown leaves. The sound of silence was crushing me, and the loneliness was overwhelming. I was feeling a pressure pressing on me; it was suffocating. I quickly realized that I had become used to people around me 24-7, and now it was a sudden cold turkey withdrawal. I was alone.

I had known of this feeling in the past and warned others of it, but never did I think it would happen to me. Fortunately, I knew what I had to do. That was to get busy or noisy. Since my work day was over, I got noisy. I ran down to the dugout, opened the door, clicked on the AM-FM radio, adjusted the dial to 101 Cash Country Music, and tuned it open full volume. Ah, people noise. This country western station was not the crying stuff either, but real fast music, thank goodness.

As promised, Jill called me that night after messages, and we had a long talk. I told her of my experience of the feeling of crushing loneliness and how I remedied it. Jill didn't laugh but understood and could relate to me about her moments of loneliness too.

For the next two days, I put in some long days in finishing the cutting of the west trail to the creek where the Hannans and I had the picnic. Cutting that trail meant I had climbed another rung on the ladder of achievements. Now knowing what was ahead of me in the cutting of the trail to Wien Lake, I decided not to do that at this time as I realized it would take months. It would be the time that I did not have remained for this year knowing I was to fly to Fairbanks the 19th of September, then drive on down the Alaskan-Canadian Highway (ALCAN) to Minnesota. Any later in driving on the ALCAN would mean early winter icy driving, and darkness.

Friday, August 27, I applied log stain on the newly converted smokehouse over to a guesthouse. After that, I added more moss on the roof of the dugout. It was soon to be the month of September. September is normally the month of the first snowfall. It was the latest time to collect the moss to add to the dugout for warmth in the coming years. Then late afternoon, precisely locate and measure where the house would be.

CHAPTER 16

Groundbreaking Ceremony

The day arrived, Friday, August 28, at 7:00 p.m., when I struck the first blow into the ground where the house was to be. With an ax in hand, I began chopping the ground cover into deep cake pan–size blocks. This chopping severed the mosses, small trees, brush, and tree roots for easier removal. The larger trees to lastly be removed before the actual excavation would begin. It was now only a groundbreaking ceremony this evening. All the while recorded on the camcorder, and then calling it a day at 8:45 p.m.

Groundbreaking ceremony

It would take the next six days to remove all the ground cover before I could begin the real excavation. These days were not long days in working on this removal because of the many other things to do at the same time. Such is the way of being a one-person company of one. Time was my enemy.

Beneath the matted ground covering thin in thickness was the yellow, rotting, vegetating materials, not like that of the black prairie sod but of gray volcanic ash and fine windblown sand. That was a developing system of the early stages of fertile soil for the first time. Neither a rock nor even a grit of stone found; I had no fear of dulling the double bit ax's sharp edge. Mind though far beneath this ash and sand was the shales that had locked within them the natural gas and oil.

To build here in the wilderness was nothing like my past life experiences of building single homes or housing developments, such as then in having to get the easements, and the building permits. That was a job by contacting the cities, to comply with their zoning laws, calling the light, water, and cable companies to locate their buried lines. All this then had to be done before I could even begin stepping into the ground a shovel's blade. In that past life, once I had the layout of the excavation staked out, the excavators would come with their machines and trucks to do their thing.

Then next day, bright and early at dawn, before the traffic would begin to fill the highways. With a three-man crew or more was depending on the size of the project. The crew and I would come the next day with smaller tools, strings, transit, stakes, and forms for the footings. Square the multi-facets of the foundation, reading the blueprints as we progressed to be sure. Then the steel reinforcing rods was brought out on a truck to be tied and hung in place before delivery of any concrete. Then at the end of the day, the concrete would be not poured but placed, filing the foundation forms. Inserting the anchor bolts where needed and then calling it a day. Organized quick and easy right?

Well, toss those dreams out the window, or in this case, over the cliff. I was alone in the middle of nowhere of my choosing, with no regrets or even a second thought. That was my dream seeing it being born in the full light of day for real. Then with my transit yet in hand, along with my tools of trade, measured and staked a

32-foot by 42-foot outline of the basement to be. Armed with years of experience of building for others, this was mine to do—mine alone with no permitting or zoning laws, but of my restricting, disciplined, perfect plan.

The excavation of the basement was to be no larger than needed to keep from anymore back filing than needed. For unpacked fill would take on more water than firm ground. By doing the excavation in this manner would make the latter waterproofing soundly sealed.

Back in 1985, the choice of building materials became clear to me, as I had walked upon the land. There was no stone nearby or even gravel for mixing concrete, of which I love to build with stone, and concrete, but here a log house it was to be. July of 1985, I had surveyed the land, so I knew I had the trees to use even though they were so far away. Trails would be made to haul the house logs to build a home. It would not be a cabin—a cabin is a one-room structure no matter the material used. But a house is of many rooms. It would be a rectangle house of three floors with central gravity heating for that most efficient system.

Walkout basements have proven to me to be the best, multipurpose and the driest of all basements. There are many advantages of a walkout, but some things would be made differently in the building of this house. For one thing, my walkout would be a drive-in plan. Having a wide enough door, not for a car or pickup truck, but for my ATVs and snow machines.

The view I choose for the house site

I had staked my land on a hillside with a two-hundred-foot immediate steep drop away gorgeous panoramic view of a valley of five lakes, and Mount Denali seventy-seven miles true south of the house to be. I had foreseen even with all the trees blocking my sight, in the month of July 1985, with first having the vision of what was to be. The land also trusted me then, and with a voice of a whispering breeze said, "Take…me…" That I did with no hesitation for it was love at first sight, between the land and me.

I researched all the books of log home plans I could find and then narrowed down the choices while back in Minnesota. There are many different methods of building a house made of logs; I studied all of them to determine the best and what was most efficient. Not the ones that looked pretty, old-fashioned, or the easiest to build, and for sure not a cabin for a weekender. But the best for holding heat and structural integrity for the ever-changing flexibility, as the logs would dry, shrink, or expand according to the season's weather conditions. Even taking into account the frequent shaking, rolling of the unannounced earthquakes that are known to occur in Alaska.

The house site was the biggest factor in the house's design. This site was on the rounded lower end of a blunted ridge that had a gradual north upslope, with an immediate sharp steep drop of two hundred feet that faced south. The sides were sharply sloping away to the east-west sides. That limited me to a thirty-foot wide house, allowing me to have a limited, narrow ATV driveway walkway combination alongside its west side to the lower south end of the house.

To save me from having to do the engineering, the making of the blueprints, I chose a known proven existing design I had found in the book *Building with Logs* by B. Allan Mackie. In fact, the photo on the cover was made by Allan Mackie's students of his, School of Log Building and Environmental Centre." That built log house on the cover is at 598 Kerry Street, Prince George, British Columbia, Canada, the Kerry Street House. This was the house I decided to build. This book, *Building with Logs*, is a very informative, interesting read, and I highly recommend it.

That book and the companion book had the plans of several log homes, *Log House Plans* by B. Allan Mackie, I had bought them both. On page 113 was the page the house plans for this house began of the two thousand square feet house. His students built a slightly different style roof; I went with the original plan and its drawings as the blueprints were out of print, but no matter, I would have no problem in working with the measurements of the detailed plans.

In a later book yet to be written as of this writing, I will be covering the house building, a ten-year building project. One thing for sure, the basement had to be of wood. I never built a wood basement before, so that I would explain how I would build it to last forever.

CHAPTER 17

Excavation and Girdling Trees

To Include Some Visitors

Time was my enemy. Today from August 29 to September 19, two rungs on my ladder of goals were yet to climb—the goals of the achievements left for me to do.

One was to have the basement dug. The other was to have as many towering white spruce trees as possible girdled—girdled for them to die and yet remain standing. To be dry before the uphill logging would begin, upon my next return. Those girdled to dry trees will make lightweight house logs, in the constructing of the basement. These dry logs would then be easier to haul, and ready to apply the penetrating preservative for their below grade placement.

For those who do not know what is meant by the term *girdling*? It first should be known. A tree gets its life-giving nutrients along with the water being drawing through its roots. All the way up under its outer bark, the tree's artery is its thick under layer or what is known as sapwood. That then distributes water to every limb, branch, twig, and leaf. This liquid substance is called sap.

Girdling trees

Girdling is by chopping completely a wide ring around the base of the tree, removing the hard outer bark, and the soft, moist sapwood beneath. By using an ax would only take time. So instead by using a chainsaw, I sawed three deep cuts to circle the tree into the harder wood and to space each of the three cuts around the trunk one inch apart. I made the three one-inch spaced apart cuts because if the lower cut heals, there then are two more cuts that further deter the tree from healing over. One cut would not be enough to kill the tree. A girdled tree dies from the top to the bottom.

Some people in secret kill a tree that is not on their property by driving in a copper spike. Why copper, I do not know. That sometimes happens because the tree or trees may be blocking a business view of the road system. Or in some cases, the trees are blocking the view of business or its sign that is hard to see from the road. Signs have to, by law, be set back a set distance from the roads right away. Tourists may otherwise drive on by an unseen sign or an establishment. A dead tree or trees then must be removed by the state, county, or township. At times rules and laws made by good intent are impediments.

When I flew the Honda 350cc ATV out to Ose Mountain on April 18, one of the items included was a snow plow blade attachment for the ATV. I had plans for this attachment to be made an earth-moving blade specifically for pushing soil to excavate the basement.

I had to modify it somewhat as it's normally for in pushing snow. Light snow at that. The four-foot wide blade was strong. But the light, weak pipe frame needed to be strengthened at the bend or elbow part of it to keep it from further bending while pushing earth or any materials of weight.

Lacking in having a welder, I come up with a way to reinforce this bend or elbows of the frame. By using a sharp pointed punch, I pounded four holes into the pipe. Two on each bend of the elbows to support 12-inch by 3/8-inch blunted point bridge spikes at a 45-degree angle of each of the elbow bends. The holes were made small only for seating the spikes in place. Once the spikes were placed, and snuggly tight, I wrapped the spike ends securely to the pipe with duct tape.

Now for the long safety springs, that allowed the blade to tilt forward when it would strike an immovable object while pushing snow. I secured the blade and vowed to make no sudden moves when pushing. This dozer worked well in that it saved me from using a wheelbarrow.

Although the dozer had no down pressure to dig in pushing loose soil, it worked great. I only had to loosen the soil by spading enough for a dozer blade full at a time, and push it off the basement site. It worked faster than I could run back and forth. I was removing material right along every day. Not like the big boys with their expensive equipment, but with what I had.

I had developed a daily routine. The first meal of the day was five pancakes of platter in size, each thickly buttered, and each layered with brown sugar. Brown sugar gave me the energy, and I believe it is a brain food. This first meal of the day gave me the highest energy I needed to last through the highly active day. I then hung my radio in a nearby tree, extended its antenna, tuned it to Cash Country 101, a radio station in Anchorage three hundred miles to the south. I turned that radio up to play loud. Alongside this radio, I hung a full two-quart canteen of water. For the suppers, at the end of the working day at nine thirty in time for messages, I made a deep kettle of hot dish that lasted for two suppers at a time. They were real spicy dishes too. I have Larry Brau to thank for those recipes.

The first thing was the removal of the ground covers before I could begin the big dig. On the second day, I only had one-third of the surface area cleared off, and the third day, three-fourths was pushed off the hill. I was working around the four big in girth birch trees, thinking, *Oh man*, to chop out those stumps with all those big roots will be a pain and take me forever. In a normal situation out in the open, I could have taken my time by building a burn pile on the tree stump's top and burn it out. That night in a dream, I had seen how to get the job done with no effort or pain.

The brain works 24-7, and during the day, my body does what the brain tells it. If I have a problem to resolve, I do it in one or two ways. Sit on a stump, and meditate for hours at a time or save the problem to dream about how to solve it. Come morning, I have dreamt the problem's solution, and go right to work on it without any further thought, but make slight adjustments as I proceed. It's like I had a connection to my ancestors that have volumes of experience. "Ask, and you shall hear. Seek, and you shall find."

To fall these four trees, I would do something never done before. The result would be the trees itself—the stumps, along with the roots, ripped out of the ground and ready to be rolled off the site effortlessly. I had to be careful, though, and use my tree falling skills. The falling of the tree's momentum and its weight would do the work for me, with no encouragement.

In this zone, even in the exposed sun's rays with no permafrost, the ground is at refrigeration temperatures even into the warm summer months. In fact, too low a temperature for anything to grow deeper than the ground cover of the surfaces mosses. There is then no tap root but only in a mass of surface roots spread out in all directions clinging to the surface's ground cover. Think about that a moment before you read on. I love a problem; this one was unique.

It's 1986 and on each, and every day, a shoulder or tripod held. The camcorder was ready for all the different opportunities of filming the various activities. During this time of the basement dig, a lot of the time the camcorder was left turned on as later on to load unedited until later, and possibly make some movie. It was a thought I had as it appears that it will never happen. At the very least, the filming recorded the sights and sounds. Now years later, with the advent of computers, DVDs, I have been able to capture photos off of the converted VHS tapes to DVDs. The DVD recordings have in the writing of my books and gave me the opportunity to insert a few select photos.

The fourth day of removing the ground cover, it was the time to record the removal of the first of the four trees.

Having a movie camera on recording me with no second takes, and live as it happens, was demanding of me not to mess this up!

Tree roots exposed

That birch was a large tree. The trunk was twenty-four inches in diameter. It would provide me with two ten-foot logs for making lumber, and the limbs would make me some fine firewood. The tree was leaning slightly. That tilt was then the way it would be fell. But before falling, I had first to do something never done before.

These trees would be as they fall, take out their roots, soil, and stump. To have that done, I would need a hurricane-force, strong wind. Or I could first sever the substantial in size roots around the tree. This tree being of the healthy size had an extensive root system. Five feet out from its base, the roots were smaller in their diameter perhaps from two to three inches. With an ax and shovel, I cut a narrow trench around the tree, keeping the same distance away from the trunk of the tree by five feet, making a perfect circle.

Of course, this took some time in chopping the roots, shoveling everything out of a trench to the cold rootless ground. This trench then was about twenty inches deep, to ensure all the roots severed.

Now it was time to do something else I had never done before, nor to my knowledge knew of anyone doing this before. I determined the favorable direction of the fall to be.

Normally a tree is fallen in this manner. The first cutting in the falling of a tree is called the bird's mouth; this would be on the side of the tree that it is to fall. A V bird's mouth if you will, a horizontal < with the bottom of the one of the two cuts being level or flat, the other sloping up. This bird's mouth cut is removed and used to direct the fall.

For starting, the trees downward fall, a back chainsaw cut is necessary, and a falling wedge inserted. The back cut is as it sounds; it is on the back side of the tree opposed to the V cut, a deep cut to place a V-shaped falling wedge after the chainsaw's bar is deep enough to clear the inserted point of the wedge. The wedges nowadays are made of hard plastic to save the chain.

The falling wedge is kept driven in tight so the tree does not come back pinching the chainsaw bar. By driving the wedge with a hammer, the tree is persuaded to fall toward the bird's mouth cut.

But in this case, there would be no back cut used on these four trees. Instead, I made an exaggerated larger than normal birds mouth. The bottom cut was flat; the sloping cut was at a 45-degree angle. All the while removing parts of this cut as I proceeded cutting into the bird's mouth. By not having a back cut in the plan, the goal was to cut deep to within two inches of severing the tree. The exaggerated wide, and deep bird's mouth, fully cleared of wood.

This unusually large cut had to be well thought through, in taking in all the considerations of the tree's size, tilt, the wind, if any, and as I cut to watch the tree for any sign of movement. I did not want the tree to pinch the chainsaw bar at all. If that happen, I would have to unbolt the bar from the chainsaw's engine, and bolt a replacement bar with chain. To use wedges as I cut away the pinched bar. Then bit by bit, cut and/or pound out removing as much as the wood I had cut to fall the tree the best I could. Ending up chopping the stump and all the roots with an ax defeating my intended plan, costing me time I did not have.

Instead by using extreme caution, my plan worked.

Tree falls

Then slowly now with the bird's mouth's wood removed, the tree began to move, then faster closing the bird's mouth wide gap tightly closed by the falling tree, with a wrenching powerful force. The tree's still-attached bending wood hinge is binding and works as a lever yanking the stump with its roots, pulling it out of the ground.

That was the reason for the 45-degree angle top cut of the bird's mouth for the maximum lever ratio. Taking into account the speed of fall, and the trees weight, all growing trees should respond in the same way. Any less of a wide angle of the exaggerated bird's mouth, the tree may stop or break the tree's hinge, leaving the stump in place.

During this cutting of the exaggerated bird's mouth, I used extreme caution and paid attention to any hint of movement or that telltale sound of a groan. Toward the end before the tree began to move, I was only touching the chainsaw into the cut, bit by bit, removing the saw each bite, being very much alert. When I detected a slight movement, I removed the saw safely to the side and ran for the camcorder that had been rolling all the while. I quickly dismounted the camcorder from the supporting tripod and placed it on my shoulder in time to record the falling action. Here are my words of the fall: "It's going…going…it's down! I bet no one has seen that before! It worked by golly."

The first tree was down as planned. After sawing off the small limbs, and piled them in a burn pile, I then cut the larger limbs into firewood lengths, stacking the wood nearby. I then cut two lumber logs and using a cant hook rolled the logs to the side of the excavation. The uprooted base and stump of the tree was on its side like that of a tipped round table. I had cut the system's root ground around the tree before the falling of this tree. It was now a simple matter of rolling the stump with its round twelve feet in diameter wheel of roots intact off the hill. That saved me an incredible amount of time.

By the way, I think for the wood artist; a stump attached to its root system could be made into a fine base for a round table leaving the choice roots for the legs.

The fifth day, in the morning, I took a handful of letters down to the trailhead for Dennis to bring back to his place in time to get them out on the plane that Chuck Philips was flying to town.

That afternoon, I began work on the falling of the seconded tree. The tree was close to falling when I had to leave it to get back to the dugout by nine thirty for messages, or a call on the CB. I was almost to the dugout when I heard the tree fall. Number 2 was now down. Upon inspection, the tree fall was a success. Thanks to a puff of wind.

Trees three and four went down too on the sixth and seventh days, all the while using extreme caution with the cleanup afterward. On the seventh day, the surface was dozed totally clear of all roots. Now the digging could begin in earnest.

On the eighth day, I set up my transit to set the height levels between the south two corners of the basement. The drop-off in front of the basement was within a few feet where I would push the basement soil over the edge, and in time, this relocation of the soil would extend the edge of the drop-off.

ATV pushes dirt over edge

I spaded the soil loose and pushed it with the ATV dozer over the edge the rest of the day. It was as though I was a kid in a sandbox having fun. At the lower end of the basement, there was less soil to remove. It was easy then for me to see I had made a lot of headway by the end of the day. Plus having a drop-off like a cliff made it easier than having to haul or toss the soil away. All this was the plan the day I drove the stake into the land claim.

The ninth day, I cut a trench four feet wide, forty-two feet long to the north end from the south end on the east edge. Digging this trench meant a lot of shoveling, tossing the soil in front of the dozer, and an equal amount of the edge down the side hill while checking the depth to keep the bottom of the trench level. Then at the end of the now nine-foot north wall of volcanic ash, I pounded in the second height stake. These stakes with a string attached then marked the level of the first trench. The ash walls were shaved straight up, and down neatly to be self-supporting. I needed no caving-in dirt wall to rework. An undermined wall may have caved in.

The tenth day, I cut a trench diagonally from the southeast corner to just east of the northwest corner. I called these two trenches slicing the pie. The aim was to divide the dig into two parts and work the trenches like they were funnels for faster, easy removal. A largely recorded portion of this work in progress is on the VHS camcorder, now on DVDs.

Mr. Bear

Every construction site has their sidewalk superintended. Today at this site was no different.

This seconded trench was nearly complete. It was far enough along that I decided to take an early advantage of removing the center portion of the basement. The ATV dozer was parked back in the trench while the radio was loudly blaring country western music; I was shoveling in the sides of the trench, piling a bulldozer's pile of soil in front of the dozer's blade.

Shoveling the trench to doze

Picture this: I am up out of the side of the trench at the shallow end of the trench, busily spading in, and shoveling tossing the soil, listening to music, when I began to sense closeness, a feeling of a presence close to my side, a sort of magnetism an energy field you might say. My left side had this feeling, the blind side of me because the eye on the left is artificially of ceramic, which is painted to match my real eye. I was not thinking much about this feeling. I kept on digging. After all, I was in the open on top a basement dig.

In the process of digging, I turned slightly to my left for a new angle in which to dig. Then instantly I felt my *heart stop*. Because six inches to my left, sat Bear. My friend, he had been sitting by my side watching me dig. Immediately with my right hand, I made a fist, and extremely hard, thumped my chest once to restart it. That all happened in an instant; I was shocked to have anything so close to my side, where there had been nothing before.

It turns out it was his emitting energy field "aura" I felt. In the same way, I do in the dark with concentration when nearby to a wall, tree, or an object. No wonder some people are nicknamed Radar. Bats use this emitting energy field to keep from flying into anything in the dark caves. The emitting energy I also use in the art of dozing.

These words spewed from my mouth in a flash. "*Geezer, Bear, you just scared the carp out of me!*" Mr. Bear turned his head and looked me in the eye, then laughed. A grunting repeated laugh, swaying, rocking from side to side, all the while at my side, he had a belly full of laughter.

He then stood up on all fours and walked over to the ATV. Bear had his eyes fixated on the ATV's soft cushy yummy seat. Bear looked at me, then at the seat, and back to me. Bear turned his face again to the soft seat and proceeded to open his mouth wide, slowly showing his long teeth. I knew then what he was about to do, and I sternly shouted "*No!*" Bear's upper two long sharp pointy teeth had just penetrated into the seat partway when I had yelled too late the no! Bear then gently withdrew his teeth. Bear turned shyly, shamefully looking back at me like he was a disciplined, bad boy.

He walked on inspecting the dig, made his way over to the lower end of the first trench, climbed out of this lower part of the trench, and came tightly up against the chalk line that I had staked for aligning the first cut. Bear turned left and walked uphill to the line and the edge of the trench. While he walked uphill, the line allowed him some slack, and he was fine until he neared the end, where the line becomes taut. He looked down into the deep trench that was at this point nine feet then back to the tightening line that was pressing him toward the trench. The upper stake that the line was attached was in his way.

Bear at this point was standing still; he was looking back and forth from the line to me. I could see his dilemma. Bear in fear of doing wrong did not want to break the line that I had so tightly strung. But also I could tell he did not know how to back down along the edge of the trench; he was afraid of falling. Imagine that, a bear afraid! I then said, in a soothing tone of voice, "That's okay, Bear. I am done with the string, go ahead."

Bear pushed into the line breaking it, *snap*, and went on over down the hill. I walked up to see where Bear had gone. There he was down by the now guest cabin, inspecting it from the outside like any sidewalk superintendent would. It had been some time since he had seen this building, perhaps days before its completion. To me, it looked like he gave it a seal of approval.

Little People

September 7, the tenth day of the dig. That is the day I discovered the Little People have a language of their own. This account is in an earlier chapter of his book, but since it was this day, I here will restate the event.

Right at seven, I was yet in my bunk. I heard outside just to the north edge of the door, two people talking to each other quietly almost in a whisper, but ever so clearly in a language, I have never heard in all my travels. The exchanges of words were clearly enunciated, and in the form of short complete sentences. It was frustrating to me that I could not understand. I do remember some words that sounded like "sokka" or like "look out" and "oogla out," realizing now I have visitors that have caught me in bed. But how could it be, I heard no planes, and I am three and a half miles from the lake?

I called to them loud enough so they could hear me. "I will be right out. I have to put some clothes on." I pulled my blue jeans, shirt, and shoes on. I did this quickly. Opened the door, and seen no one. Knowing it took me some time in getting dressed, I ran up the beaten dusty dirt path to the ridgeline. There I looked the three trails over that lead away from the dugout. Cupped my hands together, and loudly yelled, "Hey, I'm up, come on back." I called three times, each time I expected a reply. I listened for any sounds of movement or running noises. Nothing, in fact, there were no sounds. No birds, squirrels chattering, nothing, it was as quiet as an empty church. That was most unusual to hear no sounds at all.

Puzzled, I walked back down the dusty dirt path to the dugout. Going down this steep path, I was careful how I walked so as not to stumble and choose my steps carefully. It was then I see tracks. Two sets of tracks each of long strides, running uphill. The footprints were of the normal length of adult persons but shockingly were barefooted; these guys had no shoes. Their heel indents were like mine, and the five toes had no claw marks. In some of the prints, there was little sign of having an arch. Flat-footed I figured.

The prints were no larger or wider than mine, perhaps ten to eleven inches each. They were in a hurry, scuff marks mostly, but some tracks were well defined where they had begun their dash up the path.

The dusty path would not, for me, support a plaster cast mold. Maybe a spray of sorts might have, and I wished I had a good camera to take photos of the tracks.

As soon as I seen these tracks were of narrow long bare feet, I realized these two guys were Little People. I know well the footprints of a bear, and these tracks were not that of a bear.

I went on and made my breakfast, as there was nothing more I could do about what had just happened.

Back to the Dig

After eating my five usual brown sugar-coated pancakes. I continued dozing out the basement. Today the ATV used up a lot of gasoline, only thirty-five gallons left in storage. But I now have the second trench dug.

Today the fall colors were in their brightest glory. Soon perhaps in the week, a hard frost would loosen the trees of their color, and close the fall season for the coming winter's snow.

After the trench's completion, I placed wide flat boards on the ground for each wheel track, to keep from having to guess what the height the dozer's blasé should be. That, too, would maintain the integrity of the ground having no ruts made by the ATV wheels' traction. This rail system worked great; it took all the guesswork out, and time in restoring a smooth level base.

These trenches were the only place the ATV dozer was driven on in removing the soil. I shoveled every bit of the soil in front of the dozer blade. That worked by far better than using a wheelbarrow. Only after, and during final cleanup, did I scrape the floor of the basement's dig by the dozer's blade.

September 8, the fall weather was cooling fast, and the days were beginning to become shorter. This fall weather was a great motivator to get this dig done. Plus it was perfect temperature for working. All during this dig, the grouse population was becoming larger by the day; the word was out finding my digging as a place to take their baths and looking for shiny quartz crystals for their gizzards. It was like I was working in a chicken yard being careful not to drive over a chicken; they had no fear of me whatsoever. Now I know to check a grouse's gizzard for the gold quartz.

The basement hole is finished

September 13, at 4:30 p.m., I completed the digging. I am no longer using the dozer, so I removed it, stored it away, and drove to the spring for another tank of drinking water. The thought occurred to me this is the last container of water I will need this year.

Hannans Come to Visit

Early that evening, I talked to Oliver Cameron and the Hannans on the CB. It was perhaps to be my last time to be chatting with them as soon I would be leaving my mountain home. The Hannans invited themselves up to see me tomorrow to help me pack and put things away. That was so gracious of them; I looked forward to seeing them one more time. I then went fast to sleep at 7:30 p.m., where normally to sleep for me would be after midnight. It has been some interesting days, and months.

September 14, the Hannans arrived at 11:45 a.m. with the boys. The trip took them three hours and five minutes. Jill brought a treat for me, buns and cinnamon rolls, which I dearly love. They brought with them the mail for when I would leave the 19th. Together, we sawmilled 3/4-inch by 8-foot boards for them to make a toboggan or two for the boys.

At 4:00 p.m., Jill made lunch while we visited. Then we looked at the dig site, to which they were amazed to see such a big hole where there was once a hill the last time they were here.

It was that time for them to leave. Jill rode down with me, pulling the newly sawed lumber to the trailhead, and during the drive, we continued visiting. It was not easy to see them paddling away. That evening, I had a long chat with Oliver.

The Last Four Days of 1987 on Ose Mountain

September 15, and the 16th, I worked like a madman on a mission girdling trees in all parts of the woods, the box canyon, middle woods, spring area, and in the enchanted forest. As fast as I could run from tree to tree, I girdled 182 house log trees.

The Enchanted Forest, an old-growth forest, was given this name to me because each time I went through it, I was always being watched by the Little People, or the Hairy Ones. That forest and where I lived seemed to be their area's home grounds.

September 17 through the 18 was time to do the assessments, taking inventory and the making of the list. With all that done, I parked the ATV in the guest cabin, chatted on the CB, and slept in my bunk for the last time before I would return in 1988.

September 19, I dressed in my best, latched the dugouts door, gave it a look one more time, and walked down to the dock with a full pack. Then I waited a short while for Wrights Air Service to arrive to take me to Fairbanks. It was hard to leave, but now I looked forward to seeing my family again.

The plane

CHAPTER 18

Alcan Highway Drive
to Minnesota

The young pilot of Wrights Air was able to fill the plane with my empty five-gallon gasoline cans. A full plane or an empty plane costs the same. So it is always wise to have the plane full both ways. In this case, I had nothing to be hauled to me. The total cost of the flight was $485.

The pilot drove me to their company vehicle storage lot where he jumped my pickup. For the time I was on Ose Mountain, the battery had run down. It was a memory thing, I had forgotten to disconnect the battery, which had run the battery down. Therefore, I learned to disconnect the cables when parked for a long time.

From there, I checked into a room at the Klondike Inn for $48 a day. It was now the winter rates. The tourist season had ended the day schools restarted. From the room, I made calls letting my family know I was in Fairbanks and would be on the road the 21st.

The next day, the 20th, I had the wheel bearings on the two-wheel trailer replaced. I filled four five-gallon cans of gasoline for the road trip because in the remote areas in Canada, there will be some high priced gasoline, and there will be a small number of the gas stations closed for the winter. I also withdrew US cash for the trip as well as converted to an ample amount of Canadian cash. Then stopped at the Radio Station of KJNP, collected the letters they had saved for me, and wrote one letter for them to read on air to Dead Fish Lake. Then dropped in the mail for their radio that the Weronkos had requested.

The 21st, while in the town of North Pole, I bought a six-pack of soda and a bucket of crispy fried chicken for the road trip. At Tok, the last Alaskan town before the border, I filled up with gasoline. Crossed through into Canada with no hassle, and in the Yukon Territory made camp where I overlook a glacial ice field.

On the 22nd, I stopped to check the trailer axle bearings that I had a suspicion of, call it a hunch, and found they were loose. One of the axles was found rough. I had to emery cloth it to smoothen it. A passerby stopped and gave me axle grease. It is the law to stop to assist a stranded motorist on this highway, but this fellow, law or not, would have stopped all the same. I never had one bad experience with the travelers or the people residing along the way.

I am not a night driver person on roads that are without marked white lined or well-defined shoulders. For me with all the mountainous hills, and curves, I did not push my luck on such a road. The highway was without guardrails, made this way for the snow to be pushed off unobstructed. After each sunset, I pulled over and camped in some gravel pit or pullout well off the highway. The further south I traveled, the longer the daylight was, and the more improved the highway became.

But September is the last month of the year for driving on the ALCAN free of ice, and snow, at least, to the north end of this highway. Later in the winter, the snow on the road becomes dry and, it being cold, has the constancy gravel, but early in the season, it can be treacherous. I remember coming over a mountain range watching threatening weather while I drove. It was an eerie, ominous feeling. Then at the lower south end pulling in to fill up with gasoline and having the attendant tell me they just closed the highway behind me. It was closed because of a bad sudden snowstorm. I had just made it through the pass in the nick of time.

The 23rd at Watson Lake, one of the bigger towns, I filled on gasoline, stopped, and ate before driving on. Watson Lake is a good place to spend some time whether coming up to Alaska or driving south. It is a must stop.

Right after I pulled away from a Watson gas station, I saw sitting on a backpack with a sign that said Montana was a hitchhiker. No darn, it was not a pretty girl. I thought what the heck. I had the room, and it is long ways to Montana from here. We introduced ourselves and headed south. His name was Dan Harvey, from Rochester, Minnesota. Dan was a college graduate who spent the summer in Alaska at the Valdez Fish Cannery plant, which a lot of college people come to for work, and now headed back home. Dan became my camera man and a good traveling companion.

The waterfalls

When we arrived at Dawson Creek, Dan suggested driving through the British Canadian National Parks on Highway 97 to Prince George. My route usually took me through Edmonton Alberta, and on that way. Only perhaps because it had faster speed limits, with fewer hazard curves. I took his suggestion and made camp before Chetwynd. Then next day continued to Prince George. Then on Highway 16 to Jasper National Park, through Mount Robson Park, we stopped there in a scenic park and filmed the waterfalls. After we left there drove on somewhere high up in elevation where we saw the glaciers and the headwaters of the Colorado River. Wonderful views, glad we did that, drove out on 93, and then camped at Windermere.

Still on 93, we crossed into the USA, where the border guards searched through all my stuff and found a black bear gun case. It was a tanned bear skin made into a rifle case, but still they detained me until they made a call and okayed me to pass. I wondered if it was this hard to come across from Mexico. Never did I have any problems or delays crossing into Canada.

From the border crossing on to Glacier National Park at its entrance, Dan from that point would hitch a ride with some friends of his about one hundred miles away that was not in my direction of travel.

The monument for Teddy Roosevelt

Since I was here at the entrance, I drove in and viewed the sites. It was well worth the drive and to see the monument for Teddy Roosevelt.

The Painted Canyon

I followed Highway 2 east to 16, a small out of the way road off the tourist's route, and I enjoyed that. Here I got to see the real down home people of Montana; I drove this way only because I had missed Highway 13 to Glendive, and Highway 94. I finally hit 94, continued thirty-three more miles into North Dakota, and camped at a pullout tourist center on a hilltop viewpoint at 6:00 p.m., called the Painted Canyon.

Later that morning at 9:00 a.m., September 26, I drove east. Any earlier I would have had the sun direct into my face. That was a beautiful rest stop, and I took a lot of videos of it. As I was driving off out of the parking area, I was still running the camcorder. Because on the outside speaker of the tourist center was playing a pow-wow dance with the singing and the sounds of the drums, a fitting end to my visit there.

Arrived at Granite Falls at 8:30 p.m., then, of course, every trip to and from Alaska, my usual must stop is at the Granite Falls Dairy Queen, then on to Wood Lake where I see Larry Brau. He and I then got invited to Jody Berthelsen's birthday party. From there, I drove to Mom's, the Ose farm, at 10:00 p.m.

The Oses' driveway is over one-fourth of a mile. A flood of memories now flooded me as I drove up to the farm. The yard light was on, and there was light in the garage; something was up, but what?

Mom was not at home and was visiting my sister Diane in Jordan, Minnesota, but my youngest son Daniel was there.

Dan, his white-tailed buck deer, and me

Daniel and two of his hunting buddies were hanging up an eight-point white-tailed deer in the garage. After hugs and handshakes, I had to hear all about how he got this deer. Dan had with one well-placed arrow shot his deer, and because it was deep in the woods, the three of them had just brought it to the farm. It was a photo opportunity, and I had to hear from Dan all about every second of the hunt. We all were proud, how fitting of a time to have Dan get his deer.

My eldest son, David, was in the army and not home. I would drive down to Fort Hood later to see him, and his wife, Maradee, living off the post near Killeen, Texas.

The Ose farmhouse has four bedrooms, and my room was as I had left it. I slept well that night, again with my mind full of the good old days of long ago. I slept late into the next day when the phone rang downstairs. It was my daughter's mother. She came out to the farm and drove me to Marshall at 5:00 p.m. to surprise Carol at her place of work, a big ALCO store, where just that day got promoted to manager.

Her mom and I walked in like customers. As soon as I seen her, I turned on the camcorder that I held low at my side as though it was just an object but directed at Carol. Carol was busily checking the stocked shelves, dressed in a brightly colored uniform, and name tag. Her mom said, "Carol!" Carol looked at us in a state of overwhelming shock. Stood there still, dropped her hands to her sides, and cried "*Dad!*" Sobbing, but happy tears, she said, "I heard you were back. I missed you," then we hugged, and hugged with kissing too.

My daughter Carol and me hugging

Then abruptly Carol stepped back away from me and looked at me from head to foot, then said, "Dad, you're skinny!" She then placed her hands on my 36-inch waist. We hugged each other even more.

I knew then I was home.

CPSIA information can be obtained
at www.ICGtesting.com
Printed in the USA
BVHW061456070720
583137BV00007B/648